Big Data Analytics

WILEY & SAS BUSINESS SERIES

The Wiley & SAS Business Series presents books that help senior-level managers with their critical management decisions.

Titles in the Wiley and SAS Business Series include:

For more information on any of the above titles, please visit www.wiley.com.

Big Data Analytics

Turning Big Data into Big Money

Frank Ohlhorst

WILEY

John Wiley & Sons, Inc.

Library of Congress Cataloging-in-Publication Data:

Ohlhorst, Frank, 1964–
    Big data analytics : turning big data into big money / Frank Ohlhorst.
      p. cm. — (Wiley & SAS business series)
    Includes index.
    ISBN 978-1-118-14759-7 (cloth) — ISBN 978-1-118-22582-0 (ePDF) —
    ISBN 978-1-118-26380-8 (Mobi) — ISBN 978-1-118-23904-9 (ePub)
      1. Business intelligence. 2. Data mining. I. Title.
  HD38.7.O36 2013
  658.4'72—dc23

                                     2012030191

Printed in the United States of America

10 9 8 7 6 5 4 3 2 1

Contents

Preface

What are data? This seems like a simple enough question; however, depending on the interpretation, the definition of *data* can be anything from "something recorded" to "everything under the sun." Data can be summed up as everything that is experienced, whether it is a machine recording information from sensors, an individual taking pictures, or a cosmic event recorded by a scientist. In other words, everything is data. However, recording and preserving that data has always been the challenge, and technology has limited the ability to capture and preserve data.

The human brain's memory storage capacity is supposed to be around 2.5 petabytes (or 1 million gigabytes). Think of it this way: If your brain worked like a digital video recorder in a television, 2.5 petabytes would be enough to hold 3 million hours of TV shows. You would have to leave the TV running continuously for more than 300 years to use up all of that storage space. The available technology for storing data fails in comparison, creating a technology segment called *Big Data* that is growing exponentially.

Today, businesses are recording more and more information, and that information (or data) is growing, consuming more and more storage space and becoming harder to manage, thus creating Big Data. The reasons vary for the need to record such massive amounts of information. Sometimes the reason is adherence to compliance regulations, at other times it is the need to preserve transactions, and in many cases it is simply part of a backup strategy.

Nevertheless, it costs time and money to save data, even if it's only for posterity. Therein lies the biggest challenge: How can businesses continue to afford to save massive amounts of data? Fortunately, those who have come up with the technologies to mitigate these storage concerns have also come up with a way to derive value from what many see as a burden. It is a process called *Big Data analytics*.

The concepts behind Big Data analytics are actually nothing new. Businesses have been using business intelligence tools for many decades, and scientists have been studying data sets to uncover the secrets of the universe for many years. However, the scale of data collection is changing, and the more data you have available, the more information you can extrapolate from them.

The challenge today is to find the value of the data and to explore data sources in more interesting and applicable ways to develop intelligence that can drive decisions, find relationships, solve problems, and increase profits, productivity, and even the quality of life.

The key is to think big, and that means Big Data analytics.

This book will explore the concepts behind Big Data, how to analyze that data, and the payoff from interpreting the analyzed data.

Chapter 1 deals with the origins of Big Data analytics, explores the evolution of the associated technology, and explains the basic concepts behind deriving value.

Chapter 2 delves into the different types of data sources and explains why those sources are important to businesses that are seeking to find value in data sets.

Chapter 3 helps those who are looking to leverage data analytics to build a business case to spur investment in the technologies and to develop the skill sets needed to successfully extract intelligence and value out of data sets.

Chapter 4 brings the concepts of the analytics team together, describes the necessary skill sets, and explains how to integrate Big Data into a corporate culture.

Chapter 5 assists in the hunt for data sources to feed Big Data analytics, covers the various public and private sources for data, and identifies the different types of data usable for analytics.

Chapter 6 deals with storage, processing power, and platforms by describing the elements that make up a Big Data analytics system.

Chapter 7 describes the importance of security, compliance, and auditing—the tools and techniques that keep large data sources secure yet available for analytics.

Chapter 8 delves into the evolution of Big Data and discusses the short-term and long-term changes that will materialize as Big Data evolves and is adopted by more and more organizations.

Chapter 9 discusses best practices for data analysis, covers some of the key concepts that make Big Data analytics easier to deliver, and warns of the potential pitfalls and how to avoid them.

Chapter 10 explores the concept of the data pipeline and how Big Data moves through the analysis process and is then transformed into usable information that delivers value.

Sometimes the best information on a particular technology comes from those who are promoting that technology for profit and growth, hence the birth of the white paper. White papers are meant to educate and inform potential customers about a particular technology segment while gently goading those potential customers toward the vendor's product.

That said, it is always best to take white papers with a grain of salt. Nevertheless, white papers prove to be an excellent source for researching technology and have significant educational value. With that in mind, I have included the following white papers in the appendix of this book, and each offers additional knowledge for those who are looking to leverage Big Data solutions: "The MapR Distribution for Apache Hadoop" and "High Availability: No Single Points of Failure," both from MapR Technologies.

Acknowledgments

Take it from me, writing a book takes time, patience, and motivation in equal measures. At times the challenges can be overwhelming, and it becomes very easy to lose focus. However, analytics, patterns, and uncovering the hidden meaning behind data have always attracted me. When one considers the possibilities offered by comprehensive analytics and the inclusion of what may seem to be unrelated data sets, the effort involved seems almost inconsequential.

The idea for this book came from a brief conversation with John Wiley & Sons editor Timothy Burgard, who contacted me out of the blue with a proposition to build on some articles I had written on Big Data. Tim explained that comprehensive information that could be consumed by C-level executives and those entering the data analytics arena was sorely lacking, and he thought that I was up to the challenge of creating that information. So it was with Tim's encouragement that I started down the path to create a book on Big Data.

I would be remiss if I didn't mention the excellent advice and additional motivation that I received from John Wiley & Sons development editor Stacey Rivera, who was faced with the challenge of keeping me on track and moving me along in the process—a chore that I would not wish on anyone!

Putting together a book like this is a long journey that introduced me to many experts, mentors, and acquaintances who helped me to shape my ideology on how large data sets can be brought together for processing to uncover trends and other valuable bits of information.

I also have to acknowledge the many vendors in the Big Data arena who inadvertently helped me along my journey to expose the value contained in data. Those vendors, who number in the dozens, have made concentrated efforts to educate the public about the value behind Big Data, and the events they have sponsored as well as the information they have disseminated have helped to further define the market and give rise to conversations that encouraged me to pursue my ultimate goal of writing a book.

Writing takes a great deal of energy and can quickly consume all of the hours in a day. With that in mind, I have to thank the numerous editors whom I have worked with on freelance projects while concurrently writing this book. Without their understanding and flexibility, I could never have written this book, or any other. Special thanks go out to Mike Vizard, Ed Scannell, Mike Fratto, Mark Fontecchio, James Allen Miller, and Cameron Sturdevant.

When it comes to providing the ultimate in encouragement and support, no one can compare with my wife, Carol, who understood the toll that writing a book would take on family time and was still willing to provide me with whatever I needed to successfully complete this book. I also have to thank my children, Connor, Tyler, Sarah, and Katelyn, for understanding that Daddy had to work and was not always available. I am very thankful to have such a wonderful and supportive family.

CHAPTER **1**

What Is Big Data?

What exactly is *Big Data*? At first glance, the term seems rather vague, referring to something that is large and full of information. That description does indeed fit the bill, yet it provides no information on what Big Data really is.

Big Data is often described as extremely large data sets that have grown beyond the ability to manage and analyze them with traditional data processing tools. Searching the Web for clues reveals an almost universal definition, shared by the majority of those promoting the ideology of Big Data, that can be condensed into something like this: *Big Data* defines a situation in which data sets have grown to such enormous sizes that conventional information technologies can no longer effectively handle either the size of the data set or the scale and growth of the data set. In other words, the data set has grown so large that it is difficult to manage and even harder to garner value out of it. The primary difficulties are the acquisition, storage, searching, sharing, analytics, and visualization of data.

There is much more to be said about what Big Data actually is. The concept has evolved to include not only the size of the data set but also the processes involved in leveraging the data. Big Data has even become synonymous with other business concepts, such as business intelligence, analytics, and data mining.

Paradoxically, Big Data is not that new. Although massive data sets have been created in just the last two years, Big Data has its roots in the scientific and medical communities, where the complex analysis of massive amounts of data has been done for drug development, physics modeling, and other forms of research, all of which involve large data sets. Yet it is these very roots of the concept that have changed what Big Data has come to be.

THE ARRIVAL OF ANALYTICS

As analytics and research were applied to large data sets, scientists came to the conclusion that more is better—in this case, more data, more analysis, and more results. Researchers started to incorporate related data sets, unstructured data, archival data, and real-time data into the process, which in turn gave birth to what we now call Big Data.

In the business world, Big Data is all about opportunity. According to IBM, every day we create 2.5 quintillion (2.5×10^{18}) bytes of data, so much that 90 percent of the data in the world today has been created in the last two years. These data come from everywhere: sensors used to gather climate information, posts to social media sites, digital pictures and videos posted online, transaction records of online purchases, and cell phone GPS signals, to name just a few. That is the catalyst for Big Data, along with the more important fact that all of these data have intrinsic value that can be extrapolated using analytics, algorithms, and other techniques.

Big Data has already proved its importance and value in several areas. Organizations such as the National Oceanic and Atmospheric Administration (NOAA), the National Aeronautics and Space Administration (NASA), several pharmaceutical companies, and numerous energy companies have amassed huge amounts of data and now leverage Big Data technologies on a daily basis to extract value from them.

NOAA uses Big Data approaches to aid in climate, ecosystem, weather, and commercial research, while NASA uses Big Data for aeronautical and other research. Pharmaceutical companies and energy companies have leveraged Big Data for more tangible results, such as drug testing and geophysical analysis. The *New York Times* has used Big Data tools for text analysis and Web mining, while the Walt Disney Company uses them to correlate and understand customer behavior in all of its stores, theme parks, and Web properties.

Big Data plays another role in today's businesses: Large organizations increasingly face the need to maintain massive amounts of structured and unstructured data—from transaction information in data warehouses to employee tweets, from supplier records to regulatory filings—to comply with government regulations. That need has been driven even more by recent court cases that have encouraged companies to keep large quantities of documents, e-mail messages, and other electronic communications, such as instant messaging and Internet provider telephony, that may be required for e-discovery if they face litigation.

WHERE IS THE VALUE?

Extracting value is much more easily said than done. Big Data is full of challenges, ranging from the technical to the conceptual to the operational, any of which can derail the ability to discover value and leverage what Big Data is all about.

Perhaps it is best to think of Big Data in multidimensional terms, in which four dimensions relate to the primary aspects of Big Data. These dimensions can be defined as follows:

1. **Volume.** Big Data comes in one size: large. Enterprises are awash with data, easily amassing terabytes and even petabytes of information.

2. **Variety.** Big Data extends beyond structured data to include unstructured data of all varieties: text, audio, video, click streams, log files, and more.

3. **Veracity.** The massive amounts of data collected for Big Data purposes can lead to statistical errors and misinterpretation of the collected information. Purity of the information is critical for value.

4. **Velocity.** Often time sensitive, Big Data must be used as it is streaming into the enterprise in order to maximize its value to the business, but it must also still be available from the archival sources as well.

These 4Vs of Big Data lay out the path to analytics, with each having intrinsic value in the process of discovering value.

Nevertheless, the complexity of Big Data does not end with just four dimensions. There are other factors at work as well: the processes that Big Data drives. These processes are a conglomeration of technologies and analytics that are used to define the value of data sources, which translates to actionable elements that move businesses forward.

Many of those technologies or concepts are not new but have come to fall under the umbrella of Big Data. Best defined as analysis categories, these technologies and concepts include the following:

- **Traditional business intelligence (BI).** This consists of a broad category of applications and technologies for gathering, storing, analyzing, and providing access to data. BI delivers actionable information, which helps enterprise users make better business decisions using fact-based support systems. BI works by using an in-depth analysis of detailed business data, provided by databases, application data, and other tangible data sources. In some circles, BI can provide historical, current, and predictive views of business operations.

- **Data mining.** This is a process in which data are analyzed from different perspectives and then turned into summary data that are deemed useful. Data mining is normally used with data at rest or with archival data. Data mining techniques focus on modeling and knowledge discovery for predictive, rather than purely descriptive, purposes—an ideal process for uncovering new patterns from large data sets.

- **Statistical applications.** These look at data using algorithms based on statistical principles and normally concentrate on data sets related to polls, census, and other static data sets. Statistical applications ideally deliver sample observations that can be used to study populated data sets for the purpose of estimating, testing, and predictive analysis. Empirical data, such as surveys and experimental reporting, are the primary sources for ana-lyzable information.

- **Predictive analysis.** This is a subset of statistical applications in which data sets are examined to come up with predictions, based on trends and information gleaned from databases. Pre-dictive analysis tends to be big in the financial and scientific worlds, where trending tends to drive predictions, once external elements are added to the data set. One of the main goals of predictive analysis is to identify the risks and opportunities for business process, markets, and manufacturing.

■ **Data modeling.** This is a conceptual application of analytics in which multiple "what-if" scenarios can be applied via algorithms to multiple data sets. Ideally, the modeled information changes based on the information made available to the algorithms, which then provide insight to the effects of the change on the data sets. Data modeling works hand in hand with data visualization, in which uncovering information can help with a particular business endeavor.

The preceding analysis categories constitute only a portion of where Big Data is headed and why it has intrinsic value to business. That value is driven by the never-ending quest for a competitive advantage, encouraging organizations to turn to large repositories of corporate and external data to uncover trends, statistics, and other actionable information to help them decide on their next move. This has helped the concept of Big Data to gain popularity with technologists and executives alike, along with its associated tools, platforms, and analytics.

MORE TO BIG DATA THAN MEETS THE EYE

The volume and overall size of the data set is only one portion of the Big Data equation. There is a growing consensus that both semistructured and unstructured data sources contain business-critical information and must therefore be made accessible for both BI and operational needs. It is also clear that the amount of relevant unstructured business data is not only growing but will continue to grow for the foreseeable future.

Data can be classified under several categories: structured data, semistructured data, and unstructured data. Structured data are normally found in traditional databases (SQL or others) where data are organized into tables based on defined business rules. Structured data usually prove to be the easiest type of data to work with, simply because the data are defined and indexed, making access and filtering easier.

Unstructured data, in contrast, normally have no BI behind them. Unstructured data are not organized into tables and cannot be natively used by applications or interpreted by a database. A good example of unstructured data would be a collection of binary image files.

Semistructured data fall between unstructured and structured data. Semistructured data do not have a formal structure like a database with tables and relationships. However, unlike unstructured data, semi-structured data have tags or other markers to separate the elements and provide a hierarchy of records and fields, which define the data.

DEALING WITH THE NUANCES OF BIG DATA

Dealing with different types of data is converging, thanks to utilities and applications that can process the data sets using standard XML formats and industry-specific XML data standards (e.g., ACORD in insurance, HL7 in health care). These XML technologies are expanding the types of data that can be handled by Big Data analytics and integration tools, yet the transformation capabilities of these processes are still being strained by the complexity and volume of the data, leading to a mismatch between the existing transformation capabilities and the emerging needs. This is opening the door for a new type of universal data transformation product that will allow transformations to be defined for all classes of data (structured, semistructured, and unstructured), without writing code, and able to be deployed to any software application or platform architecture.

Both the definition of Big Data and the execution of the related analytics are still in a state of flux; the tools, technologies, and procedures continue to evolve. Yet this situation does not mean that those who seek value from large data sets should wait. Big Data is far too important to business processes to take a wait-and-see approach.

The real trick with Big Data is to find the best way to deal with the varied data sources and still meet the objectives of the analytical process. This takes a savvy approach that integrates hardware, software, and procedures into a manageable process that delivers results within an acceptable time frame—and it all starts with the data.

Storage is the critical element for Big Data. The data have to be stored somewhere, readily accessible and protected. This has proved to be an expensive challenge for many organizations, since network-based storage, such as SANS and NAS, can be very expensive to purchase and manage.

Storage has evolved to become one of the more pedestrian elements in the typical data center—after all, storage technologies have matured and have started to approach commodity status. Nevertheless, today's enterprises are faced with evolving needs that can put the strain on storage technologies. A case in point is the push for Big Data analytics, a concept that brings BI capabilities to large data sets.

The Big Data analytics process demands capabilities that are usually beyond the typical storage paradigms. Traditional storage technologies, such as SANS, NAS, and others, cannot natively deal with the terabytes and petabytes of unstructured information presented by Big Data. Success with Big Data analytics demands something more: a new way to deal with large volumes of data, a new storage platform ideology.

AN OPEN SOURCE BRINGS FORTH TOOLS

Enter Hadoop, an open source project that offers a platform to work with Big Data. Although Hadoop has been around for some time, more and more businesses are just now starting to leverage its capabilities. The Hadoop platform is designed to solve problems caused by massive amounts of data, especially data that contain a mixture of complex structured and unstructured data, which does not lend itself well to being placed in tables. Hadoop works well in situations that require the support of analytics that are deep and computationally extensive, like clustering and targeting.

For the decision maker seeking to leverage Big Data, Hadoop solves the most common problem associated with Big Data: storing and accessing large amounts of data in an efficient fashion.

The intrinsic design of Hadoop allows it to run as a platform that is able to work on a large number of machines that don't share any memory or disks. With that in mind, it becomes easy to see how Hadoop offers additional value: Network managers can simply buy a whole bunch of commodity servers, slap them in a rack, and run the Hadoop software on each one.

Hadoop also helps to remove much of the management overhead associated with large data sets. Operationally, as an organization's data are being loaded into a Hadoop platform, the software breaks down the data into manageable pieces and then automatically spreads them to different servers. The distributed nature of the data means there is no one place to go to access the data; Hadoop keeps track of where the data reside, and it protects the data by creating multiple copy stores. Resiliency is enhanced, because if a server goes offline or fails, the data can be automatically replicated from a known good copy.

The Hadoop paradigm goes several steps further in working with data. Take, for example, the limitations associated with a traditional centralized database system, which may consist of a large disk drive connected to a server class system and featuring multiple processors. In that scenario, analytics is limited by the performance of the disk and, ultimately, the number of processors that can be bought to bear.

With a Hadoop cluster, every server in the cluster can participate in the processing of the data by utilizing Hadoop's ability to spread the work and the data across the cluster. In other words, an indexing job works by sending code to each of the servers in the cluster, and each server then operates on its own little piece of the data. The results are then delivered back as a unified whole. With Hadoop, the process is referred to as MapReduce, in which the code or processes are mapped to all the servers and the results are reduced to a single set.

This process is what makes Hadoop so good at dealing with large amounts of data: Hadoop spreads out the data and can handle complex computational questions by harnessing all of the available cluster processors to work in parallel.

CAUTION: OBSTACLES AHEAD

Nevertheless, venturing into the world of Hadoop is not a plug-and-play experience; there are certain prerequisites, hardware requirements, and configuration chores that must be met to ensure success. The first step consists of understanding and defining the analytics process. Most chief information officers are familiar with business analytics (BA) or BI processes and can relate to the most common process layer used: the extract, transform, and load (ETL) layer and the critical role it plays when building BA or BI solutions. Big Data analytics requires that organizations choose the data to analyze, consolidate them, and then apply aggregation methods before the data can be subjected to the ETL process. This has to occur with large volumes of data, which can be structured, unstructured, or from multiple sources, such as social networks, data logs, web sites, mobile devices, and sensors.

Hadoop accomplishes that by incorporating pragmatic processes and considerations, such as a fault-tolerant clustered architecture, the ability to move computing power closer to the data, parallel and/or batch processing of large data sets, and an open ecosystem that supports enterprise architecture layers from data storage to analytics processes.

Not all enterprises require what Big Data analytics has to offer; those that do must consider Hadoop's ability to meet the challenge. However, Hadoop cannot accomplish everything on its own. Enterprises will need to consider what additional Hadoop components are needed to build a Hadoop project.

For example, a starter set of Hadoop components may consist of the following: HDFS and HBase for data management, MapReduce and OOZIE as a processing framework, Pig and Hive as development frameworks for developer productivity, and open source Pentaho for BI. A pilot project does not require massive amounts of hardware. The hardware requirements can be as simple as a pair of servers with multiple cores, 24 or more gigabytes of RAM, and a dozen or so hard disk drives of 2 terabytes each. This should prove sufficient to get a pilot project off the ground.

Data managers should be forewarned that the effective management and implementation of Hadoop requires some expertise and experience, and if that expertise is not readily available, information technology management should consider partnering with a service provider that can offer full support for the Hadoop project. Such expertise proves especially important for security; Hadoop, HDFS, and

HBase offer very little in the form of integrated security. In other words, the data still need to be protected from compromise or theft.

All things considered, an in-house Hadoop project makes the most sense for a pilot test of Big Data analytics capabilities. After the pilot, a plethora of commercial and/or hosted solutions are available to those who want to tread further into the realm of Big Data analytics.

CHAPTER 2

Why Big Data Matters

K nowing what Big Data is and knowing its value are two different things. Even with an understanding of Big Data analytics, the value of the information can still be difficult to visualize. At first glance, the well of structured, unstructured, and semistructured data seems almost unfathomable, with each bucket drawn being little more than a mishmash of unrelated data elements.

Finding what matters and why it matters is one of the first steps in drinking from the well of Big Data and the key to avoid drowning in information. However, this question still remains: Why does Big Data matter? It seems difficult to answer for small and medium businesses, especially those that have shunned business intelligence solutions in the past and have come to rely on other methods to develop their markets and meet their goals.

For the enterprise market, Big Data analytics has proven its value, and examples abound. Companies such as Facebook, Amazon, and Google have come to rely on Big Data analytics as part of their primary marketing schemes as well as a means of servicing their customers better.

For example, Amazon has leveraged its Big Data well to create an extremely accurate representation of what products a customer should buy. Amazon accomplishes that by storing each customer's searches and purchases and almost any other piece of information available, and then applying algorithms to that information to compare one customer's information with all of the other customers' information.

Amazon has learned the key trick of extracting value from a large data well and has applied performance and depth to a massive amount of data to determine what is important and what is extraneous. The company has successfully captured the data "exhaust" that any customer or potential customer has left behind to build an innovative recommendation and marketing data element.

The results are real and measurable, and they offer a practical advantage for a customer. Take, for example, a customer buying a jacket in a snowy region. Why not suggest purchasing gloves to match, or boots, as well as a snow shovel, an ice melt, and tire chains? For an in-store salesperson, those recommendations may come naturally; for Amazon, Big Data analytics is able to interpret trends and bring understanding to the purchasing process by simply looking at what customers are buying, where they are buying it, and what they have purchased in the past. Those data, combined with other public data such as census, meteorological, and even social networking data, create a unique capability that services the customer and Amazon as well.

Much the same can be said for Facebook, where Big Data comes into play for critical features such as friend suggestions, targeted ads, and other member-focused offerings. Facebook is able to accumulate information by using analytics that leverage pattern recognition, data mash-ups, and several other data sources, such as a user's preferences, history, and current activity. Those data are mined, along with the data from all of the other users, to create focused recommendations, which are reported to be quite accurate for the majority of users.

BIG DATA REACHES DEEP

Google leverages the Big Data model as well, and it is one of the originators of the software elements that make Big Data possible. However, Google's approach and focus is somewhat different from that of companies like Facebook and Amazon. Google aims to use Big Data to its fullest extent, to judge search results, predict Internet traffic usage, and service customers with Google's own applications. From the advertising perspective, Web searches can be tied to products that fit into the criteria of the search by delving into a vast mine of Web search information, user preferences, cookies, histories, and so on.

Of course, Amazon, Google, and Facebook are huge enterprises and have access to petabytes of data for analytics. However, they are not the only examples of how Big Data has affected business processes. Examples abound from the scientific, medical, and engineering communities, where huge amounts of data are gathered through experimentation, observation, and case studies. For example, the Large Hadron Collider at CERN can generate one petabyte of data per second, giving new meaning to the concept of Big Data. CERN relies on those data to determine the results of experiments using complex algorithms and analytics that can take significant amounts of time and processing power to complete.

Many pharmaceutical and medical research firms are in the same category as CERN, as well as organizations that research earthquakes, weather, and global climates. All benefit from the concept of Big Data. However, where does that leave small and medium businesses? How can these entities benefit from Big Data analytics? These businesses do not typically generate petabytes of data or deal with tremendous volumes of uncategorized data, or do they?

For small and medium businesses (SMB), Big Data analytics can deliver value for multiple business segments. That is a relatively recent development within the Big Data analytics market. Small and medium businesses have access to scores of publicly available data, including most of the Web and social networking sites. Several hosted services have also come into being that can offer the computing power, storage, and platforms for analytics, changing the Big Data analytics market into a "pay as you go, consume what you need" entity. This proves to be very affordable for the SMB market and allows those businesses to take it slow and experiment with what Big Data analytics can deliver.

OBSTACLES REMAIN

With the barriers of data volume and costs somewhat eliminated, there are still significant obstacles for SMB entities to leverage Big Data. Those obstacles include the purity of the data, analytical knowledge, an understanding of statistics, and several other philosophical and educational challenges. It all comes down to analyzing the data not just because they are there but for a specific business purpose.

For SMBs looking to gain experience in analytics, the first place to turn to is the Web—namely, for analyzing web site traffic. Here an SMB can use a tool like Blekko (http://www.blekko.com) to look at traffic distribution to a web site. This information can be very valuable for SMBs that rely on a company web site to disseminate marketing information, sell items, or communicate with current and potential customers. Blekko fits the Big Data paradigm because it looks at multiple large data sets and creates visual results that have meaningful, actionable information. Using Blekko, a small business can quickly gather statistics about its web site and compare it with a competitor's web site.

Although Blekko may be one of the simplest examples of Big Data analytics, it does illustrate the point that even in its simplest form, Big Data analytics can benefit SMBs, just as it can benefit large enterprises. Of course, other tools exist, and new ones are coming to market all of the time. As those tools mature and become accessible to the SMB market, more opportunities will arise for SMBs to leverage the Big Data concept.

Gathering the data is usually half the battle in the analytics game. SMBs can search the Web with tools like 80Legs, Extractiv, and Needlebase, all of which offer capabilities for gathering data from the Web. The data can include social networking information, sales lists, real estate listings, product lists, and product reviews and can be gathered into structured storage and then analyzed. The gathered data prove to be a valuable resource for businesses that look to analytics to enhance their market standings.

Big Data, whether done in-house or on a hosted offering, provides value to businesses of any size—from the smallest business looking to find its place in its market to the largest enterprise looking to identify the next worldwide trend. It all comes down to discovering and leveraging the data in an intelligent fashion.

The amount of data in our world has been exploding, and analyzing large data sets is already becoming a key basis of competition, underpinning new waves of productivity growth, innovation, and consumer surplus. Business leaders in every sector are going to have to deal with the implications of Big Data, either directly or indirectly.

Furthermore, the increasing volume and detail of information acquired by businesses and government agencies—paired with the rise of multimedia, social media, instant messaging, e-mail, and other Internet-enabled technologies—will fuel exponential growth in data for the foreseeable future. Some of that growth can be attributed to increased compliance requirements, but a key factor in the increase in data volumes is the increasingly sensor-enabled and instrumented world. Examples include RFID tags, vehicles equipped with GPS sensors, low-cost remote sensing devices, instrumented business processes, and instrumented web site interactions.

The question may soon arise of whether Big Data is too big, leading to a situation in which determining value may prove more difficult. This will evolve into an argument for the quality of the data over the quantity. Nevertheless, it will be almost impossible to deal with ever-growing data sources if businesses don't prepare to deal with the management of data head-on.

DATA CONTINUE TO EVOLVE

Before 2010, managing data was a relatively simple chore: Online transaction processing systems supported the enterprise's business processes, operational data stores accumulated the business transactions to support operational reporting, and enterprise data warehouses accumulated and transformed business transactions to support both operational and strategic decision making.

The typical enterprise now experiences a data growth rate of 40 to 60 percent annually, which in turn increases financial burdens and data management complexity. This situation implies that the data themselves are becoming less valuable and more of a liability for many businesses, or a low-commodity element.

Nothing could be further from the truth. More data mean more value, and countless companies have proved that axiom with Big Data analytics. To exemplify that value, one needs to look no further than at how vertical markets are leveraging Big Data analytics, which leads to a disruptive change.

For example, smaller retailers are collecting click-stream data from web site interactions and loyalty card data from traditional retailing operations. This point-of-sale information has traditionally been used by retailers for shopping basket analysis and stock replenishment, but many retailers are now going one step further and mining the data for a customer buying analysis. Those retailers are then sharing those data (after normalization and identity scrubbing) with suppliers and warehouses to bring added efficiency to the supply chain.

Another example of finding value comes from the world of science, where large-scale experiments create massive amounts of data for analysis. Big science is now paired with Big Data. There are far-reaching implications in how big science is working with Big Data; it is helping to redefine how data are stored, mined, and analyzed. Large-scale experiments are generating more data than can be held at a lab's data center (e.g., the Large Hadron Collider at CERN generates over 15 petabytes of data per year), which in turn requires that the data be immediately transferred to other laboratories for processing—a true model of distributed analysis and processing.

Other scientific quests are prime examples of Big Data in action, fueling a disruptive change in how experiments are performed and data interpreted. Thanks to Big Data methodologies, continental-scale experiments have become both politically and technologically feasible (e.g., the Ocean Observatories Initiative, the National Ecological Observatory Network, and USArray, a continental-scale seismic observatory).

Much of the disruption is fed by improved instrument and sensor technology; for instance, the Large Synoptic Survey Telescope has a 3.2-gigabyte pixel camera and generates over 6 petabytes of image data per year. It is the platform of Big Data that is making such lofty goals attainable.

The validation of Big Data analytics can be illustrated by advances in science. The biomedical corporation Bioinformatics recently announced that it has reduced the time it takes to sequence a genome from years to days, and it has also reduced the cost, so it will be feasible to sequence an individual's genome for $1,000, paving the way for improved diagnostics and personalized medicine.

The financial sector has seen how Big Data and its associated analytics can have a disruptive impact on business. Financial services firms are seeing larger volumes through smaller trading sizes, increased market volatility, and technological improvements in automated and algorithmic trading.

DATA AND DATA ANALYSIS ARE GETTING MORE COMPLEX

One of the surprising outcomes of the Big Data paradigm is the shift of where the value can be found in the data. In the past, there was an inherent hypothesis that the bulk of value could be found in structured data, which usually constitute about 20 percent of the total data stored. The other 80 percent of data is unstructured in nature and was often viewed as having limited or little value.

That perception began to change once the successes of search engine providers and e-retailers showed otherwise. It was the analysis of that unstructured data that led to click-stream analytics (for e-retailers) and search engine predictions that launched much of the Big Data movement. The first examples of the successful processing of large volumes of unstructured data led other industries to take note, which in turn has led to enterprises mining and analyzing structured and unstructured data in conjunction to look for competitive advantages.

Unstructured data bring complexity to the analytics process. Technologies such as image processing for face recognition, search engine classification of videos, and complex data integration during geospatial processing are becoming the norm in processing unstructured data. Add to that the need to support traditional transaction-based analysis (e.g., financial performance), and it becomes easy to see complexity growing exponentially. Moreover, other capabilities are becoming a requirement, such as web click-stream data driving behavioral analysis.

Behavioral analytics is a process that determines patterns of behavior from human-to-human and human-to-system interaction data. It requires large volumes of data to build an accurate model. The behavioral patterns can provide insight into which series of actions led to an event (e.g., a customer sale or a product switch). Once these patterns have been determined, they can be used in transaction processing to influence a customer's decision.

While models of transactional data analytics are well understood and much of the value is realized from structured data, it is the value found in behavioral analytics that allows the creation of a more predictive model. Behavioral interactions are less understood, and they require large volumes of data to build accurate models. This is another case where more data equal more value; this is backed by research that suggests that a sophisticated algorithm with little data is less accurate than a simple algorithm with a large amount of data. Evidence of this can be found in the algorithms used for voice and handwriting recognition and crowd sourcing.

THE FUTURE IS NOW

New developments for processing unstructured data are arriving on the scene almost daily, with one of the latest and most significant coming from the social networking site Twitter. Making sense of its massive database of unstructured data was a huge problem—so huge, in fact, that it purchased another company just to help it find the value in its massive data store. The success of Twitter revolves around how well the company can leverage the data that its users generate. This amounts to a great deal of unstructured information from the more than 200 million accounts the site hosts, which generates 230 million Twitter messages a day.

To address the problem, the social networking giant purchased BackType, the developer of Storm, a software product that can parse live data streams such as those created by the millions of Twitter feeds. Twitter has released the source code of Storm, making it available to others who want to pursue the technology. Twitter is not interested in commercializing Storm.

Storm has proved its value for Twitter, which can now perform analytics in real time and identify trends and emerging topics as they develop. For example, Twitter uses the software to calculate how widely Web addresses are shared by multiple Twitter users in real time.

With the capabilities offered by Storm, a company can process Big Data in real time and garner knowledge that leads to a competitive advantage. For example, calculating the reach of a Web address could take up to 10 minutes using a single machine. However, with a Storm cluster, that workload can be spread out to dozens of machines, and a result can be discovered in just seconds. For companies that make money from emerging trends (e.g., ad agencies, financial services, and Internet marketers), that faster processing can be crucial.

Like Twitter, many organizations are discovering that they have access to a great deal of data, and those data, in all forms, could be transformed into information that can improve efficiencies, maximize profits, and unveil new trends. The trick is to organize and analyze the data quickly enough, a process that can now be accomplished using open source technologies and lumped under the heading of Big Data.

Other examples abound of how unstructured, semistructured, and structured Big Data stores are providing value to business segments. Take, for example, the online shopping service LivingSocial, which leverages technologies such as the Apache Hadoop data processing platform to garner information about what its users want.

The process has allowed LivingSocial to offer predictive analysis in real time, which better services its customer base. The company is not alone in its quest for squeezing the most value out of its unstructured data. Other major shopping sites, shopping comparison sites, and online versions of brick-and-mortar stores have also implemented technologies to bring real-time analytics to the forefront of customer interaction.

However, in that highly competitive market, finding new ways to interpret the data and process them faster is proving to be the critical competitive advantage and is driving Big Data analytics forward with new innovations and processes. Those enterprises and many others learned that data in all forms cannot be considered a commodity item, and just as with gold, it is through mining that one finds the nuggets of value that can affect the bottom line.

CHAPTER 3

Big Data and the Business Case

Big Data is quickly becoming more than just a buzzword. A plethora of organizations have made significant investments in the technology that surrounds Big Data and are currently starting to leverage the content within to find real value.

Even so, there is still a great deal of confusion about Big Data, similar to what many information technology (IT) managers have experienced in the past with disruptive technologies. Big Data is disruptive in the way that it changes how business intelligence (BI) is used in a business—and that is a scary proposition for many senior executives.

That situation puts chief technology officers, chief information officers, and IT managers in the unenviable position of trying to prove that a disruptive technology will actually improve business operations. Further complicating this situation is the high cost associated with in-house Big Data processing, as well as the security concerns that surround the processing of Big Data analytics off-site.

Perhaps some of the strife comes from the term *Big Data* itself. Nontechnical people may think of Big Data literally, as something associated with big problems and big costs. Presenting Big Data as "Big Analytics" instead may be the way to win over apprehensive decision makers while building a business case for the staff, technology, and results that Big Data relies upon.

The trick is to move beyond the accepted definition of Big Data—which implies that it is nothing more than data sets that have become too large to manage with traditional tools—and explain that Big Data is a combination of technologies that mines the value of large databases.

And *large* is the key word here, simply because massive amounts of data are being collected every second—more than ever imaginable—and the size of these data is greater than can be practically managed by today's current strategies and technologies.

That has created a revolution in which Big Data has become centered on the tsunami of data and how it will change the execution of businesses processes. These changes include introducing greater efficiencies, building new processes for revenue discovery, and fueling innovation. *Big Data* has quickly grown from a new buzzword being tossed around technology circles into a practical definition for what it is really all about, Big Analytics.

REALIZING VALUE

A number of industries—including health care, the public sector, retail, and manufacturing—can obviously benefit from analyzing their rapidly growing mounds of data. Collecting and analyzing transactional data gives organizations more insight into their customers' preferences, so the data can then be used as a basis for the creation of products and services. This allows the organizations to remedy emerging problems in a timely and more competitive manner.

The use of Big Data analytics is thus becoming a key foundation for competition and growth for individual firms, and it will most likely underpin new waves of productivity, growth, and consumer surplus.

THE CASE FOR BIG DATA

Building an effective business case for a Big Data project involves identifying several key elements that can be tied directly to a business process and are easy to understand as well as quantify. These elements are knowledge discovery, actionable information, short-term and long-term benefits, the resolution of pain points, and several others that are aligned with making a business process better by providing insight.

In most instances, Big Data is a disruptive element when introduced into an enterprise, and this disruption includes issues of scale, storage, and data center design. The disruption normally involves costs associated with hardware, software, staff, and support, all of which affect the bottom line. That means that return on investment (ROI) and total cost of ownership (TCO) are key elements of a Big Data business plan. The trick is to accelerate ROI while reducing TCO. The simplest way to do this is to associate a Big Data business plan with other IT projects driven by business needs.

While that might sound like a real challenge, businesses are actually investing in storage technologies and improved processing to meet other business goals, such as compliance, data archiving, cloud initiatives, and continuity planning. These initiatives can provide the foundation for a Big Data project, thanks to the two primary needs of Big Data: storage and processing.

Lately the natural growth of business IT solutions has been focused on processes that take on a distributed nature in which storage and applications are spread out over multiple systems and locations. This also proves to be a natural companion to Big Data, further helping to lay the foundation for Big Analytics.

Building a business case involves using case scenarios and providing supporting information. An extensive supply of examples exists, with several draft business cases, case scenarios, and other collateral, all courtesy of the major vendors involved with Big Data solutions. Notable vendors with massive amounts of collateral include IBM, Oracle, and HP.

While there is no set formula for building a business case, there are some critical elements that can be used to define how a business case should look, which helps to ensure the success of a Big Data project.

A solid business case for Big Data analytics should include the following:

- **The complete background of the project.** This includes the drivers of the project, how others are using Big Data, what business processes Big Data will align with, and the overall goal of implementing the project.
- **Benefits analysis.** It is often difficult to quantify the benefits of Big Data as static and tangible. Big Data analytics is all about the

interpretation of data and the visualization of patterns, which amounts to a subjective analysis, highly dependent on humans to translate the results. However, that does not prevent a business case from including benefits driven by Big Data in nonsubjective terms (e.g., identifying sales trends, locating possible inventory shrinkage, quantifying shipping delays, or measuring customer satisfaction). The trick is to align the benefits of the project with the needs of a business process or requirement. An example of that would be to identify a business goal, such as 5 percent annual growth, and then show how Big Data analytics can help to achieve that goal.

■ **Options.** There are several paths to take to the destination of Big Data, ranging from in-house big iron solutions (data centers running large mainframe systems) to hosted offerings in the cloud to a hybrid of the two. It is important to research these options and identify how each may work for achieving Big Data analytics, as well as the pros and cons of each. Preferences and benefits should also be highlighted, allowing a financial decision to be tied to a technological decision.

■ **Scope and costs.** Scope is more of a management issue than a physical deployment issue. It all comes down to how the implementation scope affects the resources, especially personnel and staff. Scope questions should identify the *who* and the *when* of the project, in which personnel hours and technical expertise are defined, as well as the training and ancillary elements. Costs should also be associated with staffing and training issues, which helps to create the big picture for TCO calculations and provides the basis for accurate ROI calculations.

■ **Risk analysis.** Calculating risk can be a complex endeavor. However, since Big Data analytics is truly a business process that provides BI, risk calculations can include the cost of doing nothing compared to the benefits delivered by the technology. Other risks to consider are security implications (where the data live and who can access it), CPU overhead (whether the analytics will limit the processing power available for a line of business applications), compatibility and integration issues (whether the installation and operation will work with the existing technology), and disruption of business processes (installation creates downtime). All of these elements can be considered risks with a large-scale project and should be accounted for to build a solid business case.

Of course, the most critical theme of a business case is ROI. The return, or benefit, that an organization is likely to receive in relation to the cost of the project is a ratio that can change as more research is done and information is gathered while building a business case. Ideally, the ROI-to-cost ratio improves as more research is done and the business case writers discover additional value from the implementation of a Big Data analytics solution. Nevertheless, ROI is usually the most important factor in determining whether a project will ultimately go forward. The determination of ROI has become one of the primary reasons that companies and nonprofit organizations engage in the business case process in the first place.

THE RISE OF BIG DATA OPTIONS

Teradata, IBM, HP, Oracle, and many other companies have been offering terabyte-scale data warehouses for more than a decade, but those offerings were tuned for processes in which data warehousing was the primary goal. Today, data tend to be collected and stored in a wider variety of formats and can include structured, semistructured, and unstructured elements, which each tend to have different storage and management requirements. For Big Data analytics, data must be able to be processed in parallel across multiple servers. This is a necessity, given the amounts of information being analyzed.

In addition to having exhaustively maintained transactional data from databases and carefully culled data residing in data warehouses, organizations are reaping untold amounts of log data from servers and forms of machine-generated data, customer comments from internal and external social networks, and other sources of loose, unstructured data.

Such data sets are growing at an exponential rate, thanks to Moore's Law. Moore's Law states that the number of transistors that can be placed on a processor wafer doubles approximately every 18 months. Each new generation of processors is twice as powerful as its most recent predecessor. Similarly, the power of new servers also doubles every 18 months, which means their activities will generate correspondingly larger data sets.

The Big Data approach represents a major shift in how data are handled. In the past, carefully culled data were piped through the network to a data warehouse, where they could be further examined. However, as the volume of data increases, the network becomes a bottleneck. That is the kind of situation in which a distributed platform, such as Hadoop, comes into play. Distributed systems allow the analysis to occur where the data reside.

Traditional data systems are not able to handle Big Data effectively, either because those systems are not designed to handle the variety of today's data, which tend to have much less structure, or because the data systems cannot scale quickly and affordably. Big Data analytics works very differently from traditional BI, which normally relies on a clean subset of user data placed in a data warehouse to be queried in a limited number of predetermined ways.

Big Data takes a very different approach, in which all of the data an organization generates are gathered and interacted with. That allows administrators and analysts to worry about how to use the data later. In that sense, Big Data solutions prove to be more scalable than traditional databases and data warehouses.

To understand how the options around Big Data have evolved, one must go back to the birth of Hadoop and the dawn of the Big Data movement. Hadoop's roots can be traced back to a 2004 Google white paper that described the infrastructure Google built to analyze data on many different servers, using an indexing system called Bigtable. Google kept Bigtable for internal use, but Doug Cutting, a developer who had already created the Lucene and Solr open source search engine, created an open source version of Bigtable, naming the technology Hadoop after his son's stuffed elephant.

One of Hadoop's first adopters was Yahoo, which dedicated large amounts of engineering work to refine the technology around 2006. Yahoo's primary challenge was to make sense of the vast amount of interesting data stored across separated systems. Unifying those data and analyzing them as a whole became a critical goal for Yahoo, and Hadoop turned out to be an ideal platform to make that happen. Today Yahoo is one of the biggest users of Hadoop and has deployed it on more than 40,000 servers.

The company uses the technology for multiple business cases and analytics chores. Yahoo's Hadoop clusters hold massive log files of what stories and sections users click on; advertisement activity is also stored, as are lists of all of the content and articles Yahoo publishes. For Yahoo, Hadoop has proven to be well suited for searching for patterns in large sets of text.

BEYOND HADOOP

Another name to become familiar with in the Big Data realm is the Cassandra database, a technology that can store 2 million columns in a single row. That makes Cassandra ideal for appending more data onto existing user accounts without knowing ahead of time how the data should be formatted.

Cassandra's roots can also be traced to an online service provider, in this case Facebook, which needed a massive distributed database to power the service's inbox search. Like Yahoo, Facebook wanted to use the Google Bigtable architecture, which could provide a column- and row-oriented database structure that could be spread on a large number of nodes.

However, Bigtable had a serious limitation: It used a master node–oriented design. Bigtable depended on a single node to coordinate all read-and-write activities on all of the nodes. This meant that if the head node went down, the whole system would be useless.

Cassandra was built on a distributed architecture called Dynamo, which the Amazon engineers who developed it described in a 2007 white paper. Amazon uses Dynamo to keep track of what its millions of online customers are putting in their shopping carts.

Dynamo gave Cassandra an advantage over Bigtable, since Dynamo is not dependent on any one master node. Any node can accept data for the whole system, as well as answer queries. Data are replicated on multiple hosts, creating resiliency and eliminating the single point of failure.

WITH CHOICE COME DECISIONS

Many of the tools first developed by online service providers are becoming more available for enterprises as open source software. These days, Big Data tools are being tested by a wider range of organizations, beyond the large online service providers. Financial institutions, telecommunications, government agencies, utility companies, retail, and energy companies all are testing Big Data systems.

Naturally, more choices can make a decision harder, which is perhaps one of the biggest challenges associated with putting together a business plan that meets project needs while not introducing any additional uncertainty into the process. Ideally, a Big Data business plan will exemplify the primary goal of supporting both long-term strategic analysis and one-off transactional and behavioral analysis, which delivers both immediate benefits and long-term benefits.

While Hadoop is applicable to the majority of businesses, it is not the only game in town (at least when it comes to open source implementations). Once an organization has decided to leverage its heaps of machine-generated and social networking data, setting up the infrastructure will not be the biggest challenge. The biggest challenge may come from deciding to go it alone with an open source or to turn to one of the commercial implementations of Big Data technology. Vendors such as Cloudera, Hortonworks, and MapR are commercializing Big Data technologies, making them easier to deploy and manage.

Add to that the growing crop of Big Data on-demand services from cloud services providers, and the decision process becomes that much more complex. Decision makers will have to invest in research and perform due diligence to select the proper platform and implementation methodology to make a business plan successful. However, most of that legwork can be done during the business plan development phase, when the pros and cons of the various Big Data methodologies can be weighed and then measured against the overall goals of the business plan. Which technology will get there the fastest, with the lowest cost, and without mortgaging future capabilities?

CHAPTER 4

Building the Big Data Team

One of the most important elements of a Big Data project is a rather obvious but often overlooked item: people. Without human involvement or interpretation, Big Data analytics becomes useless, having no purpose and no value. It takes a team to make Big Data work, and even if that team consists of only two individuals, it is still a necessary element.

Bringing people together to build a team can be an arduous process that involves multiple meetings, perhaps recruitment, and, of course, personnel management. Several specialized skills in Big Data are required, and that is what defines the team. Determining those skills is one of the first steps in putting a team together.

THE DATA SCIENTIST

One of the first concepts to become acquainted with is the data scientist; a relatively new title, it is not readily recognized or accepted by many organizations, but it is here to stay.

A data scientist is normally associated with an employee or a business intelligence (BI) consultant who excels at analyzing data, particularly large amounts of data, to help a business gain a competitive edge. The data scientist is usually the de facto team leader during a Big Data analytics project.

The title *data scientist* is sometimes disparaged because it lacks specificity and can be perceived as an aggrandized synonym for *data analyst*. Nevertheless, the position is gaining acceptance with large enterprises that are interested in deriving meaning from Big Data, the voluminous amount of structured, unstructured, and semistructured data that a large enterprise produces or has access to.

A data scientist must possess a combination of analytic, machine learning, data mining, and statistical skills as well as experience with algorithms and coding. However, the most critical skill a data scientist should possess is the ability to translate the significance of data in a way that can be easily understood by others.

THE TEAM CHALLENGE

Finding and hiring talented workers with analytics skills is the first step in creating an effective data analytics team. Organizing that team is the next step; the relationship between IT and BI groups must be incorporated into the team design, leading to a determination of how much autonomy to give to Big Data analytics professionals.

Enterprises with highly organized and centralized corporate structures will lean toward placing an analytics team under an IT department or a business intelligence competency center. However, many experts have found that successful Big Data analytics projects seem to work better using a less centralized approach, giving team members the freedom to interpret results and define new ways of looking at data.

For maximum effectiveness, Big Data analytics teams can be organized by business function or placed directly within a specific business unit. An example of this would be placing an analytics team that focuses on customer churn (the turnover of customer accounts) and other marketing-related analysis in a marketing department, while a risk-focused data analytics project team would be better suited to a finance department.

Ideally, placing the Big Data analytics team into a department where the resulting data have immediate value is the best way to accelerate findings, determine value, and deliver results in an actionable fashion. That way the analyst and the departmental decision makers are speaking the same language and working in a collaborative fashion to eke out the best results.

It all depends on scale. A small business may have different analytical needs than a large business does, and that obviously affects the relationship with the data analysis professionals and the departments they work with.

DIFFERENT TEAMS, DIFFERENT GOALS

A case in point would be an engineering firm that is examining large volumes of unstructured data for a technical analysis. The firm itself may be quite small, but the data set may be quite large. For example, if an engineering firm was designing a bridge, the components of Big Data analytics could involve everything from census data to traffic patterns to weather factors, which could be used to uncover load and traffic trends that would affect the design of the bridge. If other elements are added, such as market data (materials costs and anticipated financial growth for the area), the definition of a data scientist may change. That individual may need an engineering background and a keen understanding of economics and may work only with the primary engineers on the project and not with any other company departments.

This can mean that the firm's marketing and sales departments are left out in the cold. The question then is how important is that style of analytics to those departments—arguably, it is not important at all. In a situation like that, market analysis, competition, government funding, infrastructure age and usage, and population density may not be as applicable to the in-place data scientist but may require a different individual skill set to successfully interpret the results.

As analytics needs and organizational size increase, roles may change, as well as the processes and the relationships involved. Larger organizations tend to have the resources and budgets to better leverage their data. In those cases, it becomes important to recognize the primary skills needed by a Big Data analytics team and to build the team around core competencies. Fortunately, it is relatively easy to identify those core competencies, because the tasks of the team can be broken down into three capabilities.

DON'T FORGET THE DATA

There are three primary capabilities needed in a data analytics team: (1) locating the data, (2) normalizing the data, and (3) analyzing the data.

For the first capability, locating the data, an individual has to be able to find relevant data from internal and external sources and work with the IT department's data governance team to secure access to the data. That individual may also need to work with external businesses, government agencies, and research firms to gain access to large data sets, as well as understand the difference between structured and unstructured data.

For the second capability, normalizing the data, an individual has to prepare the raw data before they are analyzed to remove any spurious data. This process requires technical skills as well as analytics skills. The individual may also need to know how to combine the data sets, load those data sets on the storage platform, and build a matrix of fields to normalize the contents.

The third capability, analyzing the data, is perhaps the team's most important chore. For most organizations, the analytic process is con- ducted by the data scientist, who accesses the data, designs algorithms, gathers the results, and then presents the information.

These three primary chores define a data analytics team's func- tions. However, there are several subsets of tasks that fall under each category, and these tasks can vary based on scope and other elements specific to the required data analytics process.

Much like the data themselves, the team should not be static in nature and should be able to evolve and adapt to the needs of the business.

CHALLENGES REMAIN

Locating the right talent to analyze data is the biggest hurdle in building a team. Such talent is in high demand, and the need for data analysts and data scientists continues to grow at an almost exponential rate.

Finding this talent means that organizations will have to focus on data science and hire statistical modelers and text data–mining pro- fessionals as well as people who specialize in sentiment analysis.

Success with Big Data analytics requires solid data models, statistical predictive models, and test analytic models, since these will be the core applications needed to do Big Data.

Locating the appropriate talent takes more than just a typical IT job placement; the skills required for a good return on investment are not simple and are not solely technology oriented. Some organizations may turn to consulting firms to meet the need for talent; however, many consulting firms also have trouble finding the experts that can make Big Data pay off.

Nevertheless, there is a silver lining to the Big Data storm cloud. Big Data is about business as much as it is about technology, which means that it requires a hybrid talent. This allows the pool of potential experts to be much deeper than just the IT professional workforce. In fact, a Big Data expert could be developed from other departments that are not IT centered but that do have a significant need for research, analysis, and interpretation of facts.

The potential talent pool may grow to include any staffers who have an inherent interest in the Big Data technology platforms in play, who have a tools background from web site development work earlier in their careers, or who are just naturally curious, talented, and self-taught in a quest to be better at their jobs. These are typically individuals who can understand the value of data and the ideology of how to interpret the data.

But organizations should not hire just anyone who shows a spark of interest in or a basic understanding of data analytics. It is important to develop a litmus test of sorts to determine if an individual has the appropriate skills to succeed in what may be a new career. The candidates should possess a foundation of five critical skills to immediately bring value to a Big Data team:

1. Data mining
2. Data visualization
3. Data analysis
4. Data manipulation
5. Data discovery

These define what a data scientist should be able to accomplish.

TEAMS VERSUS CULTURE

Arguably, finding and hiring talented workers with analytics skills is the first step in establishing an advanced data analytics team. If that is indeed the case, then the second step would be determining how to structure the team in relation to existing IT and BI groups, as well as determining how much autonomy to give the analytics professionals.

That process may require building a new culture of technology professionals who also have significant business skills. Developing that culture depends on many factors, such as making sure that the teams are educated in the ways of the business culture in place and emphasizing measurements and results.

Starting at the top proves to be one of the best ways to transform an IT-centered culture into an internal business culture that thrives on advanced data analytics technology and fact-based decision making. Businesses that have experienced a change in senior management often clear the path for the development of a data analytics business culture and a data warehousing, BI, and advanced analytics program.

Instituting a change in cultural ideology is one of the most important chores associated with leveraging analytics. Many companies have become accustomed to running operations based on gut feelings and what has worked in the past, both of which lead to a formulaic way of conducting business.

Nowhere has this been more evident than in major retail chains, which usually pride themselves on consistency across locations. That cultural perspective can prove to be the antithesis of a dynamic, competitive business. Instituting a culture that uses the ideology of analytics can transform business operations. For example, the business can better serve markets by using data mining and predictive analytics tools to automatically set plans for placing inventory into individual retail locations. The key is putting the needed products in front of potential customers, such as by knowing that snow shovels will not sell in Florida and that suntan lotion sells poorly in Alaska.

Another potential way to foster an analytics business culture within an organization is to set up a dedicated data analytics group. An analytics group with its own director could develop an analytics strategy and project plan, promote the use of analytics within the company, train data analysts on analytics tools and concepts, and work with the IT, BI, and data warehousing teams on deployment projects.

GAUGING SUCCESS

Success has to be measured, and measuring a team's contribution to the bottom line can be a difficult process. That is why it is important to build objectives, measurements, and milestones that demonstrate the benefits of a team focused on Big Data analytics. Developing performance measurements is an important part of designing a business plan. With Big Data, those metrics can be assigned to the specific goal in mind.

For example, if an organization is looking to bring efficiency to a warehouse, a performance metric may be measuring the amount of empty shelf space and what the cost of that empty shelf space means to the company. Analytics can be used to identify product movement, sales predictions, and so forth to move product into that shelf space to better service the needs of customers. It is a simple comparison of the percentage of space used before the analytics process and the percentage of space used after the analytics team has tackled the issue.

CHAPTER **5**

Big Data Sources

One of the biggest challenges for most organizations is finding data sources to use as part of their analytics processes. As the name implies, Big Data is large, but size is not the only concern. There are several other considerations when deciding how to locate and parse Big Data sets.

The first step is to identify usable data. While that may be obvious, it is anything but simple. Locating the appropriate data to push through an analytics platform can be complex and frustrating. The source must be considered to determine whether the data set is appropriate for use. That translates into detective work or investigative reporting.

Considerations should include the following:

- Structure of the data (structured, unstructured, semistructured, table based, proprietary)
- Source of the data (internal, external, private, public)
- Value of the data (generic, unique, specialized)
- Quality of the data (verified, static, streaming)
- Storage of the data (remotely accessed, shared, dedicated platforms, portable)
- Relationship of the data (superset, subset, correlated)

All of those elements and many others can affect the selection process and can have a dramatic effect on how the raw data are prepared ("scrubbed") before the analytics process takes place.

In the IT realm, once a data source is located, the next step is to import the data into an appropriate platform. That process may be as simple as copying data onto a Hadoop cluster or as complicated as scrubbing, indexing, and importing the data into a large SQL-type table. That importation, or gathering of the data, is only one step in a multistep, sometimes complex process.

Once the importation (or real-time updating) has been performed, templates and scripts can be designed to ease further data-gathering chores. Once the process has been designed, it becomes easier to execute in the future.

Building a Big Data set ultimately serves one strategic purpose: to mine the data, or dig for something of value. Mining data involves a lot more than just running algorithms against a particular data source. Usually, the data have to be first imported into a platform that can deal with the data in an appropriate fashion. This means the data have to be transformed into something accessible, queryable, and relatable. Mining starts with a mine or, in Big Data parlance, a platform. Ultimately, to have any value, that platform must be populated with usable information.

HUNTING FOR DATA

Finding data for Big Data analytics is part science, part investigative work, and part assumption. Some of the most obvious sources for data are electronic transactions, web site logs, and sensor information. Any data the organization gathers while doing business are included. The idea is to locate as many data sources as possible and bring the data into an analytics platform. Additional data can be gathered using network taps and data replication clients. Ideally, the more data that can be captured, the more data there will be to work with.

Finding the internal data is the easy part of Big Data. It gets more complicated once data considered unrelated, external, or unstructured are bought into the equation. With that in mind, the big question with Big Data now is, "Where do I get the data from?" This is not easily answered; it takes some research to separate the wheat from the chaff, knowing that the chaff may have some value as well.

Setting out to build a Big Data warehouse takes a concentrated effort to find the appropriate data. The first step is to determine what Big Data analytics is going to be used for. For example, is the business looking to analyze marketing trends, predict web traffic, gauge customer satisfaction, or achieve some other lofty goal that can be accomplished with the current technologies?

It is this knowledge that will determine where and how to gather Big Data. Perhaps the best way to build such knowledge is to better understand the business analytics (BA) and business intelligence (BI) processes to determine how large-scale data sets can be used to interact with internal data to garner actionable results.

SETTING THE GOAL

Every project usually starts out with a goal and with objectives to reach that goal. Big Data analytics should be no different. However, defining the goal can be a difficult process, especially when the goal is vague and amounts to little more than something like "using the data better." It is imperative to define the goal before hunting for data sources, and in many cases, proven examples of success can be the foundation for defining a goal.

Take, for example, a retail organization. The goal for Big Data analytics may be to increase sales, a chore that spans several business ideologies and departments, including marketing, pricing, inventory, advertising, and customer relations. Once there is a goal in mind, the next step is to define the objectives, the exact means by which to reach the goal.

For a project such as the retail example, it will be necessary to gather information from a multitude of sources, some internal and others external. Some of the data may have to be purchased, and some may be available under the public domain. The key is to start with the internal, structured data first, such as sales logs, inventory movement, registered transactions, customer information, pricing, and supplier interactions.

Next come the unstructured data, such as call center and support logs, customer feedback (perhaps e-mails and other communications), surveys, and data gathered by sensors (store traffic, parking lot usage).

The list can include many other internally tracked elements; however, it is critical to be aware of diminishing returns on investment with the data sourced. In other words, some log information may not be worth the effort to gather, because it will not affect the analytics outcome.

Finally, external data must be taken into account. There is a vast wealth of external information that can be used to calculate everything from customer sentiments to geopolitical issues. The data that make up the public portion of the analytics process can come from government entities, research companies, social networking sites, and a multitude of other sources.

For example, a business may decide to mine Twitter, Facebook, the U.S. census, weather information, traffic pattern information, and news archives to build a complex source of rich data. Some controls need to be in place, and that may even include scrubbing the data before processing (i.e., removing spurious information or invalid elements).

The richness of the data is the basis for predictive analytics. A company looking to increase sales may compare population trends, along with social sentiment, to customer feedback and satisfaction to identify where the sales process could be improved. The data warehouse can be used for much more after the initial processing, and real-time data could also be integrated to identify trends as they arise.

The retail situation is only one example; there are dozens of others, each of which may have a specific applicability to the task at hand.

BIG DATA SOURCES GROWING

Multiple sources are responsible for a growth in data that is applicable to Big Data technology. Some of these sources represent entirely new data sources, while others are a change in the resolution of the existing data generated. Much of that growth can be attributed to industry digitization of content.

With companies now turning to creating digital representations of existing data and acquiring everything that is new, data growth rates over the last few years have been nearly infinite, simply because most of the businesses involved started from zero.

Many industries fall under the umbrella of new data creation and digitization of existing data, and most are becoming appropriate sources for Big Data resources. Those industries include the following:

- **Transportation, logistics, retail, utilities, and telecommunications.** Sensor data are being generated at an accelerating rate from fleet GPS transceivers, RFID (radio-frequency identification) tag readers, smart meters, and cell phones (call data records); these data are used to optimize operations and drive operational BI to realize immediate business opportunities.

- **Health care.** The health care industry is quickly moving to electronic medical records and images, which it wants to use for short-term public health monitoring and long-term epidemiological research programs.

- **Government.** Many government agencies are digitizing public records, such as census information, energy usage, budgets, Freedom of Information Act documents, electoral data, and law enforcement reporting.

- **Entertainment media.** The entertainment industry has moved to digital recording, production, and delivery in the past five years and is now collecting large amounts of rich content and user viewing behaviors.

- **Life sciences.** Low-cost gene sequencing (less than $1,000) can generate tens of terabytes of information that must be analyzed to look for genetic variations and potential treatment effectiveness.

- **Video surveillance.** Video surveillance is still transitioning from closed-caption television to Internet protocol television cameras and recording systems that organizations want to analyze for behavioral patterns (security and service enhancement).

For many businesses, the additional data can come from self-service marketplaces, which record the use of affinity cards and track the sites visited, and can be combined with social networks and location-based metadata. This creates a goldmine of actionable consumer data for retailers, distributors, and manufacturers of consumer packaged goods.

The legal profession is adding to the multitude of data sources, thanks to the discovery process, which is dealing more frequently with electronic records and requiring the digitization of paper documents for faster indexing and improved access. Today, leading e-discovery companies are handling terabytes or even petabytes of information that need to be retained and reanalyzed for the full course of a legal proceeding.

Additional information and large data sets can be found on social media sites such as Facebook, Foursquare, and Twitter. A number of new businesses are now building Big Data environments, based on scale-out clusters using power-efficient multicore processors that leverage consumers' (conscious or unconscious) nearly continuous streams of data about themselves (e.g., likes, locations, and opinions).

Thanks to the network effect of successful sites, the total data generated can expand at an exponential rate. Some companies have collected and analyzed over 4 billion data points (e.g., web site cut-and-paste operations) since information collection started, and within a year the process has expanded to 20 billion data points gathered.

DIVING DEEPER INTO BIG DATA SOURCES

A change in resolution is further driving the expansion of Big Data. Here additional data points are gathered from existing systems or with the installation of new sensors that deliver more pieces of information. Some examples of increased resolution can be found in the following areas:

- **Financial transactions.** Thanks to the consolidation of global trading environments and the increased use of programmed trading, the volume of transactions being collected and analyzed is doubling or tripling. Transaction volumes also fluctuate much faster, much wider, and much more unpredictably. Competition among firms is creating more data, simply because sampling for trading decisions is occurring more frequently and at faster intervals.

■ **Smart instrumentation.** The use of smart meters in energy grid systems, which shifts meter readings from monthly to every 15 minutes, can translate into a multithousandfold increase in data generated. Smart meter technology extends beyond just power usage and can measure heating, cooling, and other loads, which can be used as an indicator of household size at any given moment.

■ **Mobile telephony.** With the advances in smartphones and connected PDAs, the primary data generated from these devices have grown beyond caller, receiver, and call length. Additional data are now being harvested at exponential rates, including elements such as geographic location, text messages, browsing history, and (thanks to the addition of accelerometers) even motions, as well as social network posts and application use.

A WEALTH OF PUBLIC INFORMATION

For those looking to sample what is available for Big Data analytics, a vast amount of data exists on the Web; some of it is free, and some of it is available for a fee. Much of it is simply there for the taking. If your goal is to start gathering data, it is pretty hard to beat many of the tools that are readily available on the market. For those looking for point-and-click simplicity, Extractiv (http://www.extractiv.com) and Mozenda (http://www.mozenda.com) offer the ability to acquire data from multiple sources and to search the Web for information.

Another candidate for processing data on the Web is Google Refine (http://code.google.com/p/google-refine), a tool set that can work with messy data, cleaning them up and then transforming them into different formats for analytics. 80Legs (http://www.80legs.com) specializes in gathering data from social networking sites as well as retail and business directories.

The tools just mentioned are excellent examples for mining data from the Web to transform them into a Big Data analytics platform. However, gathering data is only the first of many steps. To garner value from the data, they must be analyzed and, better yet, visualized. Tools such as Grep (http://www.linfo.org/grep.html), Turk (http://www.mturk.com), and BigSheets (http://www-01.ibm.com/software/

ebusiness/jstart/bigsheets) offer the ability to analyze data. For visualization, analysts can turn to tools such as Tableau Public (http://www.tableausoftware.com), OpenHeatMap (http://www.openheatmap.com), and Gephi (http://www.gephi.org).

Beyond the use of discovery tools, Big Data can be found through services and sites such as CrunchBase, the U.S. census, InfoChimps, Kaggle, Freebase, and Timetric. Many other services offer data sets directly for integration into Big Data processing.

The prices of some of these services are rather reasonable. For example, you can download a million Web pages through 80Legs for less than three dollars. Some of the top data sets can be found on commercial sites, yet for free. An example is the Common Crawl Corpus, which has crawl data from about five billion Web pages and is available in the ARC file format from Amazon S3. The Google Books Ngrams is another data set that Amazon S3 makes available for free. The file is in a Hadoop-friendly format. For those who may be wondering, n-grams are fixed-size sets of items. In this case, the items are words extracted from the Google Books corpus. The n specifies the number of elements in the set, so a five-gram contains five words or characters.

Many more data sets are available from Amazon S3, and it is definitely worth visiting http://aws.amazon.com/publicdatasets/ to track these down. Another site to visit for a listing of public data sets is http://www.quora.com/Data/Where-can-I-get-large-datasets-open-to-the-public, a treasure trove of links to data sets and information related to those data sets.

GETTING STARTED WITH BIG DATA ACQUISITION

Barriers to Big Data adoption are generally cultural rather than technological. In particular, many organizations fail to implement Big Data programs because they are unable to appreciate how data analytics can improve their core business. One the most common triggers for Big Data development is a data explosion that makes existing data sets very large and increasingly difficult to manage with conventional database management tools.

As these data sets grow in size—typically ranging from several terabytes to multiple petabytes—businesses face the challenge of capturing, managing, and analyzing the data in an acceptable time frame. Getting started involves several steps, starting with training. Training is a prerequisite for understanding the paradigm shift that Big Data offers. Without that insider knowledge, it becomes difficult to explain and communicate the value of data, especially when the data are public in nature. Next on the list is the integration of development and operations teams (known as DevOps), the people most likely to deal with the burdens of storing and transforming the data into something usable.

Much of the process of moving forward will lie with the business executives and decision makers, who will also need to be brought up to speed on the value of Big Data. The advantages must be explained in a fashion that makes sense to the business operations, which in turn means that IT pros are going to have to do some legwork. To get started, it proves helpful to pursue a few ideologies:

- Identify a problem that business leaders can understand and relate to and that commands their attention.

- Do not focus exclusively on the technical data management challenge. Be sure to allocate resources to understand the uses for the data within the business.

- Define the questions that must be answered to meet the business objective, and only then focus on discovering the necessary data.

- Understand the tools available to merge the data and the business process so that the result of the data analysis is more actionable.

- Build a scalable infrastructure that can handle growth of the data. Good analysis requires enough computing power to pull in and analyze data. Many people get discouraged because when they start the analytic process, it is slow and laborious.

- Identify technologies that you can trust. A dizzying variety of open source Big Data software technologies are available, and many are likely to disappear within a few years. Find one that has professional vendor support, or be prepared to take on permanent maintenance of the technology as well as the solution in the long run. Hadoop seems to be attracting a lot of mainstream vendor support.

■ Choose a technology that fits the problem. Hadoop is best for large but relatively simple data set filtering, converting, sorting, and analysis. It is also good for sifting through large volumes of text. It is not really useful for ongoing persistent data management, especially if structural consistency and transactional integrity are required.

■ Be aware of changing data formats and changing data needs. For instance, a common problem faced by organizations seeking to use BI solutions to manage marketing campaigns is that those campaigns can be very specifically focused, requiring an analysis of data structures that may be in play for only a month or two. Using conventional relational database management system techniques, it can take several weeks for database administrators to get a data warehouse ready to accept the changed data, by which time the campaign is nearly over. A MapReduce solution, such as one built on a Hadoop framework, can reduce those weeks to a day or two. Thus it is not just volume but also variety that can drive Big Data adoption.

ONGOING GROWTH, NO END IN SIGHT

Data creation is occurring at a record rate. In fact, the research firm IDC's Digital Universe Study predicts that between 2009 and 2020, digital data will grow 44-fold, to 35 zettabytes per year. It is also important to recognize that much of this data explosion is the result of an explosion in devices located at the periphery of the network, including embedded sensors, smartphones, and tablet computers. All of these data create new opportunities for data analytics in human genomics, health care, oil and gas, search, surveillance, finance, and many other areas.

CHAPTER 6

The Nuts and Bolts of Big Data

A ssembling a Big Data solution is sort of like putting together an erector set. There are various pieces and elements that must be put together in the proper fashion to make sure everything works adequately, and there are almost endless combinations of configurations that can be made with the components at hand.

With Big Data, the components include platform pieces, servers, virtualization solutions, storage arrays, applications, sensors, and routing equipment. The right pieces must be picked and integrated in a fashion that offers the best performance, high efficiency, affordability, ease of management and use, and scalability.

THE STORAGE DILEMMA

Big Data consists of data sets that are too large to be acquired, handled, analyzed, or stored in an appropriate time frame using the traditional infrastructures. *Big* is a term relative to the size of the organization and, more important, to the scope of the IT infrastructure that's in place. The scale of Big Data directly affects the storage platform that must be put in place, and those deploying storage solutions have to understand that Big Data uses storage resources differently than the typical enterprise application does.

These factors can make provisioning storage a complex endeavor, especially when one considers that Big Data also includes analysis; this is driven by the expectation that there will be value in all of the information a business is accumulating and a way to draw that value out.

Originally driven by the concept that storage capacity is inexpensive and constantly dropping in price, businesses have been compelled to save more data, with the hope that business intelligence (BI) can leverage the mountains of new data created every day. Organizations are also saving data that have already been analyzed, which can potentially be used for marking trends in relation to future data collections.

Aside from the ability to store more data than ever before, businesses also have access to more *types* of data. These data sources include Internet transactions, social networking activity, automated sensors, mobile devices, scientific instrumentation, voice over Internet protocol, and video elements. In addition to creating static data points, transactions can create a certain velocity to this data growth. For example, the extraordinary growth of social media is generating new transactions and records. But the availability of ever-expanding data sets doesn't guarantee success in the search for business value.

As data sets continue to grow with both structured and unstructured data and data analysis becomes more diverse, traditional enterprise storage system designs are becoming less able to meet the needs of Big Data. This situation has driven storage vendors to design new storage platforms that incorporate block- and file-based systems to meet the needs of Big Data and associated analytics.

Meeting the challenges posed by Big Data means focusing on some key storage ideologies and understanding how those storage design elements interact with Big Data demands, including the following:

- **Capacity.** Big Data can mean petabytes of data. Big Data storage systems must therefore be able to quickly and easily change scale to meet the growth of data collections. These storage systems will need to add capacity in modules or arrays that are transparent to users, without taking systems down. Most Big Data environments are turning to scale-out storage (the ability to increase storage performance as capacity increases) technologies to meet that criterion. The clustered architecture of scale-out storage solutions features nodes of storage capacity with embedded processing power and connectivity that can grow seamlessly, avoiding the silos of storage that traditional systems can create.

Big Data also means many large and small files. Managing the accumulation of metadata for file systems with multiple large and small files can reduce scalability and impact performance, a situation that can be a problem for traditional network-attached storage systems. Object-based storage architectures, in contrast, can allow Big Data storage systems to expand file counts into the billions without suffering the overhead problems that traditional file systems encounter. Object-based storage systems can also scale geographically, enabling large infrastructures to be spread across multiple locations.

■ **Security.** Many types of data carry security standards that are driven by compliance laws and regulations. The data may be financial, medical, or government intelligence and may be part of an analytics set yet still be protected. While those data may not be different from what current IT managers must accommodate, Big Data analytics may need to cross-reference data that have not been commingled in the past, and this can create some new security considerations. In turn, IT managers should consider the security footing of the data stored in an array used for Big Data analytics and the people who will access the data.

■ **Latency.** In many cases, Big Data employs a real-time component, especially in use scenarios involving Web transactions or financial transactions. An example is tailoring Web advertising to each user's browsing history, which demands real-time analytics to function. Storage systems must be able to grow rapidly and still maintain performance. Latency produces "stale" data. That is another case in which scale-out architectures solve problems. The technology enables the cluster of storage nodes to increase in processing power and connectivity as they grow in capacity. Object-based storage systems can parallel data streams, further improving output.

Most Big Data environments need to provide high input-output operations per second (IOPS) performance, especially those used in high-performance computing environments. Virtualization of server resources, which is a common methodology used to expand compute resources without the purchase of new hardware, drives high IOPS requirements, just as it does in traditional IT environments. Those high IOPS performance requirements can be met with solid-state storage devices, which can be implemented in many different formats, including simple server-based cache to all-flash-based scalable storage systems.

■ **Access.** As businesses get a better understanding of the potential of Big Data analysis, the need to compare different data sets increases, and with it, more people are bought into the data sharing loop. The quest to create business value drives businesses to look at more ways to cross-reference different data objects from various platforms. Storage infrastructures that include global file systems can address this issue, since they allow multiple users on multiple hosts to access files from many different back-end storage systems in multiple locations.

■ **Flexibility.** Big Data storage infrastructures can grow very large, and that should be considered as part of the design challenge, dictating that care should be taken in the design and allowing the storage infrastructure to grow and evolve along with the analytics component of the mission. Big Data storage infrastructures also need to account for data migration challenges, at least during the start-up phase. Ideally, data migration will become something that is no longer needed in the world of Big Data, simply because the data are distributed in multiple locations.

■ **Persistence.** Big Data applications often involve regulatory compliance requirements, which dictate that data must be saved for years or decades. Examples are medical information, which is often saved for the life of the patient, and financial information, which is typically saved for seven years. However, Big Data users are often saving data longer because they are part of a historical record or are used for time-based analysis. The requirement for longevity means that storage manufacturers need to include ongoing integrity checks and other long-term reliability features as well as address the need for data-in-place upgrades.

- **Cost.** Big Data can be expensive. Given the scale at which many organizations are operating their Big Data environments, cost containment is imperative. That means more efficiency as well as less expensive components. Storage deduplication has already entered the primary storage market and, depending on the data types involved, could bring some value for Big Data storage systems. The ability to reduce capacity consumption even by a few percentage points provides a significant return on investment as data sets grow. Other Big Data storage technologies that can improve efficiencies are thin provisioning, snapshots, and cloning.

- Thin provisioning operates by allocating disk storage space in a flexible manner among multiple users based on the minimum space required by each user at any given time.

- Snapshots streamline access to stored data and can speed up the process of data recovery. There are two main types of storage snapshot: copy-on-write (or low-capacity) snapshot and split-mirror snapshot. Utilities are available that can automatically generate either type.

- Disk cloning is copying the contents of a computer's hard drive. The contents are typically saved as a disk image file and transferred to a storage medium, which could be another computer's hard drive or removable media such as a DVD or a USB drive.

Data storage systems have evolved to include an archive component, which is important for organizations that are dealing with historical trends or long-term retention requirements. From a capacity and dollar standpoint, tape is still the most economical storage medium. Today, systems that support multiterabyte cartridges are becoming the de facto standard in many of these environments.

The biggest effect on cost containment can be traced to the use of commodity hardware. This is a good thing, since the majority of Big Data infrastructures won't be able to rely on the big iron enterprises of the past. Most of the first and largest Big Data users have built their own "white-box" systems on-site, which leverage a commodity-oriented, cost-saving strategy.

These examples and others have driven the trend of cost containment, and more storage products are arriving on the market that are software based and can be installed on existing systems or on common, off-the-shelf hardware. In addition, many of the same vendors are selling their software technologies as commodity appliances or partnering with hardware manufacturers to produce similar offerings. That all adds up to cost-saving strategies, which brings Big Data into the reach of smaller and smaller businesses.

- **Application awareness.** Initially, Big Data implementations were designed around application-specific infrastructures, such as custom systems developed for government projects or the white-box systems engineered by large Internet service companies. Application awareness is becoming common in mainstream storage systems and should improve efficiency or performance, which fits right into the needs of a Big Data environment.

- **Small and medium business.** The value of Big Data and the associated analytics is trickling down to smaller organizations, which creates another challenge for those building Big Data storage infrastructures: creating smaller initial implementations that can scale yet fit into the budgets of smaller organizations.

BUILDING A PLATFORM

Like any application platform, a Big Data application platform must support all of the functionality required for any application platform, including elements such as scalability, security, availability, and continuity.

Yet Big Data Application platforms are unique; they need to be able to handle massive amounts of data across multiple data stores and initiate concurrent processing to save time. This means that a Big Data platform should include built-in support for technologies such as MapReduce, integration with external Not only SQL (NoSQL) databases, parallel processing capabilities, and distributed data services. It should also make use of the new integration targets, at least from a development perspective.

Consequently, there are specific characteristics and features that a Big Data platform should offer to work effectively with Big Data analytics processes:

- **Support for batch and real-time analytics.** Most of the existing platforms for processing data were designed for handling transactional Web applications and have little support for business analytics applications. That situation has driven Hadoop to become the de facto standard for handling batch processing. However, real-time analytics is altogether different, requiring something more than Hadoop can offer. An event-processing framework needs to be in place as well. Fortunately, several technologies and processing alternatives exist on the market that can bring real-time analytics into Big Data platforms, and many major vendors, such as Oracle, HP, and IBM, are offering the hardware and software to bring real-time processing to the forefront. However, for the smaller business that may not be a viable option because of the cost. For now, real-time processing remains a function that is provided as a service via the cloud for smaller businesses.

- **Alternative approaches.** Transforming Big Data application development into something more mainstream may be the best way to leverage what is offered by Big Data. This means creating a built-in stack that integrates with Big Data databases from the NoSQL world and creating MapReduce frameworks such as Hadoop and distributed processing. Development should account for the existing transaction-processing and event-processing semantics that come with the handling of the real-time analytics that fit into the Big Data world.

Creating Big Data applications is very different from writing a typical "CRUD application" (create, retrieve, update, delete) for a centralized relational database. The primary difference is with the design of the data domain model, as well as the API and Query semantics that will be used to access and process that data. Mapping is an effective approach in Big Data, hence the success of MapReduce, in which there is an impedance mismatch between different data models and sources. An appropriate example is the use of object and relational mapping tools like Hibernate for building a bridge between the impedance mismatches.

■ **Available Big Data mapping tools.** Batch-processing projects are being serviced with frameworks such as Hive, which provide an SQL-like facade for handling complex batch processing with Hadoop. However, other tools are starting to show promise. An example is JPA, which provides a more standardized JEE abstraction that fits into real-time Big Data applications. The Google app Engine uses Data Nucleus along with Bigtable to achieve the same goal, while GigaSpaces uses OpenJPA's JPA abstraction combined with an in-memory data grid. Red Hat takes a different approach and leverages Hibernate object-grid mapping to map Big Data.

■ **Big Data abstraction tools.** There are several choices available to abstract data, ranging from open source tools to commercial distributions of specialized products. One to pay attention to is Spring Data from SpringSource, which is a high-level abstraction tool that offers the ability to map different data stores of all kinds into one common abstraction through annotation and a plug-in approach.

Of course, one of the primary capabilities offered by abstraction tools is the ability to normalize and interpret the data into a uniform structure, which can be further worked with. The key here is to make sure that whatever abstraction technology is employed deals with current and future data sets efficiently.

■ **Business logic.** A critical component of the Big Data analytics process is logic, especially business logic, which is responsible for processing the data. Currently, MapReduce reigns supreme in the realm of Big Data business logic. MapReduce was designed to handle the processing of massive amounts of data through moving the processing logic to the data and distributing the logic in parallel to all nodes. Another factor that adds to the appeal of MapReduce is that developing parallel processing code is very complex.

When designing a custom Big Data application platform, it is critical to make MapReduce and parallel execution simple. That can be accomplished by mapping the semantics into existing programming models. An example is to extend an existing model, such as SessionBean, to support the needed semantics. This makes parallel processing look like a standard invocation of single-job execution.

- **Moving away from SQL.** SQL is a great query language. However, it is limited, at least in the realm of Big Data. The problem lies in the fact that SQL relies on a schema to work properly, and Big Data, especially when it is unstructured, does not work well with schema-based queries. It is the dynamic data structure of Big Data that confounds the SQL schema-based processes. Here Big Data platforms must be able to support schema-less semantics, which in turn means that the data mapping layer would need to be extended to support document semantics. Examples are MongoDB, CouchBase, Cassandra, and the GigaSpaces document API. The key here is to make sure that Big Data application platforms support more relaxed versions of those semantics, with a focus on providing flexibility in consistency, scalability, and performance.

- **In-memory processing.** If the goal is to deliver the best performance and reduce latency, then one must consider using RAM-based devices and perform processing in-memory. However, for that to work effectively, Big Data platforms need to provide a seamless integration between RAM and disk-based devices in which data that are written in RAM would be synched into the disk asynchronously. Also, the platforms need to provide common abstractions that allow users the same data access API for both devices and thus make it easier to choose the right tool for the job without changing the application code.

- **Built-in support for event-driven data distribution.** Big Data applications (and platforms) must also be able to work with event-driven processes. With Big Data, this means there must be data awareness incorporated, which makes it easy to route messages based on data affinity and the content of the message. There also have to be controls that allow the creation of fine-grained semantics for triggering events based on data operations (such as add, delete, and update) and content, as with complex event processing.

- **Support for public, private, and hybrid clouds.** Big Data applications consume large amounts of computer and storage resources. This has led to the use of the cloud and its elastic capabilities for running Big Data applications, which in turn can offer a more economical approach to processing Big Data jobs. To take advantage of those economics, Big Data application platforms must include built-in support for public, private, and hybrid clouds that will include seamless transitions between the various cloud platforms through integration with the available frameworks. Examples abound, such as JClouds and Cloud Bursting, which provides a hybrid model for using cloud resources as spare capacity to handle load.

- **Consistent management.** The typical Big Data application stack incorporates several layers, including the database itself, the Web tier, the processing tier, caching layer, the data synchronization and distribution layer, and reporting tools. A major disadvantage for those managing Big Data applications is that each of those layers comes with different management, provisioning, monitoring, and troubleshooting tools. Add to that the inherent complexity of Big Data applications, and effective management, along with the associated maintenance, becomes difficult.

With that in mind, it becomes critical to choose a Big Data application platform that integrates the management stack with the application stack. An integrated management capability is one of the best productivity elements that can be incorporated into a Big Data platform.

Building a Big Data platform is no easy chore, especially when one considers that there may be a multitude of right ways and wrong ways to do it. This is further complicated by the plethora of tools, technologies, and methodologies available. However, there is a bright side that stresses flexibility, and since Big Data is constantly evolving, flexibility will rule in building a custom platform or choosing one off the shelf.

BRINGING STRUCTURE TO UNSTRUCTURED DATA

In its native format, a large pile of unstructured data has little value. It is burdensome in the typical enterprise, especially one that has not adopted Big Data practices to extract the value.

However, extracting value can be akin to finding a needle in a haystack, and if that haystack is spread across several farms and the needle is in pieces, it becomes even more difficult. One of the primary jobs of Big Data analytics is to piece that needle back together and organize the haystack into a single entity to speed up the search. That can be a tall order with unstructured data, a type of data that is growing in volume and size as well as complexity.

Unstructured (or uncatalogued) data can take many forms, such as historical photograph collections, audio clips, research notes, genealogy materials, and other riches hidden in various data libraries. The Big Data movement has driven methodologies to create dynamic and meaningful links among these currently unstructured information sources.

For the most part, that has resulted in the creation of metadata and methods to bring structure to unstructured data. Currently, two dominant technical and structural approaches have emerged: (1) a reliance on search technologies, and (2) a trend toward automated data categorization. Many data categorization techniques are being applied across the landscape, including taxonomies, semantics, natural language recognition, auto-categorization, "what's related" functionality, data visualization, and personalization. The idea is to provide the information that is needed to process an analytics function.

The importance of integrating structured and loosely unstructured data cannot be overstated in the world of Big Data analytics. There are a few enabling technical strategies that make it possible to sort the wheat from the chaff. For instance, there is SQL-NoSQL Integration. Those using MapReduce and other schemaless frameworks have been struggling with structural data and analytics coming from the relational database management system (RDBMS) side. However, the integration of the relational and nonrelational paradigms provides the most powerful analytics by bringing together the best of both worlds.

There are several technologies that enable this integration; some of them take advantage of the processing power of MapReduce frameworks like Hadoop to perform data transformation in place, rather than doing it in a separate middle tier. Some tools combine this capability with in-place transformation at the target database as well, taking advantage of the computing capabilities of engineered machines and using change data capture to synchronize, source, and target, again without the overhead of a middle tier. In both cases, the overarching principle is real-time data integration, in which reflecting data change instantly in a data warehouse—whether originating from a MapReduce job or from a transactional system—and create downstream analytics that have an accurate, timely view of reality. Others are turning to linked data and semantics, where data sets are created using linking methodologies that focus on the semantics of the data.

This fits well into the broader notion of pointing at external sources from within a data set, which has been around for quite a long time. That ability to point to unstructured data (whether residing in the file system or some external source) merely becomes an extension of the given capabilities, in which the ability to store and process XML and XQuery natively within an RDBMS enables the combination of different degrees of structure while searching and analyzing the underlying data.

Newer semantics technologies can take this further by providing a set of formalized XML-based standards for storage, querying, and manipulation of data. Since these technologies have been focused on the Web, many businesses have not associated the process with Big Data solutions.

Most NoSQL technologies fall into the categories of key value stores, graph, or document databases; the semantic resource description framework (RDF) triple store creates an alternative. It is not relational in the traditional sense, but it still maintains relationships between data elements, including external ones, and does so in a flexible, extensible fashion.

A record in an RDF store is composed of a *triple*, consisting of subject, predicate, and object. That does not impose a relational schema on the data, which supports the addition of new elements without structural modifications to the store. In addition, the underlying system can resolve references by inferring new triples from the existing records using a rules set. This is a powerful alternative to joining relational tables to resolve references in a typical RDBMS, while also offering a more expressive way to model data than a key value store.

One of the most powerful aspects of semantic technology comes from the world of linguistics and natural language processing, also known as entity extraction. This is a powerful mechanism to extract information from unstructured data and combine it with transactional data, enabling deep analytics by bringing these worlds closer together.

Another method that brings structure to the unstructured is the text analytics tool, which is improving daily as scientists come up with new ways of making algorithms understand written text more accurately. Today's algorithms can detect names of people, organizations, and locations within seconds simply by analyzing the context in which words are used. The trend for this tool is to move toward recognition of further useful entities, such as product names, brands, events, and skills.

Entity relation extraction is another important tool, in which a relation that consistently connects two entities in many documents is important information in science and enterprise alike. Entity relation extraction detects new knowledge in Big Data. Other unstructured data tools are detecting sentiment in social data, integrating multiple languages, and applying text analytics to audio and video transcripts. The number of videos is growing at a constant rate, and transcripts are even more unstructured than written text because there is no punctuation.

PROCESSING POWER

Analyzing Big Data can take massive amounts of processing power. There is a simple relationship between data analytics and processing power: the larger the data set and the faster that results are needed, the more processing power it takes. However, processing Big Data analytics is not a simple matter of throwing the latest and fastest processor at the problem; it is more about the ideology behind grid-computing technologies.

Big Data involves more than just distributed processing technologies, like Hadoop. It is also about faster processors, wider bandwidth communications, and larger and cheaper storage to achieve the goal of making the data consumable. That in turn drives the idea of data visualization and interface technologies, which make the results of analysis consumable by humans, and that is where the raw processing power comes to bear for analytics.

Intuitiveness comes from proper analysis, and proper analysis requires the appropriate horsepower and infrastructure to mine an appropriate data set from huge piles of data. To that end, distributed processing platforms such as Hadoop and MapReduce are gaining favor over big iron in the realm of Big Data analytics.

Perhaps the simplest argument for pursuing a distributed infrastructure is the flexibility of scale, in which more commodity hardware can just be thrown at a particular analysis project to increase performance and speed results. That distributed ideology plays well into grid processing and cloud-based services, which can be employed as needed to process data sets.

The primary thing to remember about building a processing platform for Big Data is how processing can scale. For example, many businesses start off small, with a few commodity PCs running a Hadoop-based platform, but as the amount of data and the available sources grow exponentially, the ability to process the data falls exponentially, meaning that designs must incorporate a look-ahead methodology. That is where IT professionals will need to consider available, future technologies to scale processing to their needs.

Cloud-based solutions that offer elastic-type services are a decent way to future-proof a Big Data analytics platform, simply because of the ability of a cloud service to instantly scale to the loads placed upon it.

There is no simple answer to how to process Big Data with the technology choices available today. Nevertheless, major vendors are looking to make the choices easier by providing canned solutions that are based on appliance models, while others are building complete cloud-based Big Data solutions to meet the elastic needs of small and medium businesses looking to leverage Big Data.

CHOOSING AMONG IN-HOUSE, OUTSOURCED, OR HYBRID APPROACHES

The world of Big Data is filled with choices—so many that most IT professionals can become overwhelmed with options, technologies, and platforms. It is almost at the point at which Big Data analytics is required to choose among the various Big Data ideologies, platforms, and tools.

However, the question remains of where to start with Big Data. The answer can be found in how Big Data systems evolve or grow. In the past, working with Big Data always meant working on the scale of a dedicated data center. However, commodity hardware using platforms like Hadoop has changed the dynamic, decreasing storage prices, and open source applications have further lowered the initial cost of entry. These new dynamics allow smaller businesses to experiment with Big Data and then expand the platforms as needed as successes are built.

Once a pilot project has been constructed using open source software with commodity hardware and storage devices, IT managers can then measure how well the pilot platform meets their needs. Only after the processing needs and volume of data increase can an IT manager make a decision on where to head with a Big Data analytics platform, developing one in-house or turning to the cloud.

CHAPTER 7

Security, Compliance, Auditing, and Protection

The sheer size of a Big Data repository brings with it a major security challenge, generating the age-old question presented to IT: How can the data be protected? However, that is a trick question—the answer has many caveats, which dictate how security must be imagined as well as deployed. Proper security entails more than just keeping the bad guys out; it also means backing up data and protecting data from corruption.

The first caveat is access. Data can be easily protected, but only if you eliminate access to the data. That's not a pragmatic solution, to say the least. The key is to control access, but even then, knowing the *who*, *what*, *when*, and *where* of data access is only a start.

The second caveat is availability: controlling where the data are stored and how the data are distributed. The more control you have, the better you are positioned to protect the data.

The third caveat is performance. Higher levels of encryption, complex security methodologies, and additional security layers can all improve security. However, these security techniques all carry a processing burden that can severely affect performance.

The fourth caveat is liability. Accessible data carry with them liability, such as the sensitivity of the data, the legal requirements connected to the data, privacy issues, and intellectual property concerns.

Adequate security in the Big Data realm becomes a strategic balancing act among these caveats along with any additional issues the caveats create. Nonetheless, effective security is an obtainable, if not perfect, goal. With planning, logic, and observation, security becomes manageable and omnipresent, effectively protecting data while still offering access to authorized users and systems.

PRAGMATIC STEPS TO SECURING BIG DATA

Securing the massive amounts of data that are inundating organizations can be addressed in several ways. A starting point is to basically get rid of data that are no longer needed. If you do not need certain information, it should be destroyed, because it represents a risk to the organization. That risk grows every day for as long as the information is kept. Of course, there are situations in which information cannot legally be destroyed; in that case, the information should be securely archived by an offline method.

The real challenge may be determining whether the data are needed—a difficult task in the world of Big Data, where value can be found in unexpected places. For example, getting rid of activity logs may be a smart move from a security standpoint. After all, those seeking to compromise networks may start by analyzing activity so they can come up with a way to monitor and intercept traffic to break into a network. In a sense, those logs present a serious risk to an organization, and to prevent the logs from being exposed, the best method may be to delete them after their usefulness ends.

However, those logs could be used to determine scale, use, and efficiency of large data systems, an analytical process that falls right under the umbrella of Big Data analytics. Here a catch-22 is created: Logs are a risk, but analyzing those logs properly can mitigate risks as well. Should you keep or dispose of the data in these cases?

There is no easy answer to that dilemma, and it becomes a case of choosing the lesser of two evils. If the data have intrinsic value for analytics, they must be kept, but that does not mean they need to be kept on a system that is connected to the Internet or other systems. The data can be archived, retrieved for processing, and then returned to the archive.

CLASSIFYING DATA

Protecting data becomes much easier if the data are classified—that is, the data should be divided into appropriate groupings for management purposes. A classification system does not have to be very sophisticated or complicated to enable the security process, and it can be limited to a few different groups or categories to keep things simple for processing and monitoring.

With data classification in mind, it is essential to realize that all data are not created equal. For example, Internal e-mails between two colleagues should not be secured or treated the same way as financial reports, human resources (HR)information, or customer data.

Understanding the classifications and the value of the data sets is not a one-task job; the life-cycle management of data may need to be shared by several departments or teams in an enterprise. For example, you may want to divide the responsibilities among technical, security, and business organizations. Although it may sound complex, it really isn't all that hard to educate the various corporate shareholders to understand the value of data and where their responsibilities lie.

Classification can become a powerful tool for determining the sensitivity of data. A simple approach may just include classifications such as financial, HR, sales, inventory, and communications, each of which is self-explanatory and offers insight into the sensitivity of the data.

Once organizations better understand their data, they can take important steps to segregate the information, which will make the deployment of security measures like encryption and monitoring more manageable. The more data are placed into silos at higher levels, the easier it becomes to protect and control them. Smaller sample sizes are easier to protect and can be monitored separately for specific necessary controls.

PROTECTING BIG DATA ANALYTICS

It is sad to report that protecting data is an often forgotten inclination in the data center, an afterthought that falls behind current needs. The launch of Big Data initiatives is no exception in the data center, and protection is too often an afterthought. Big Data offers more of a challenge than most other data center technologies, making it the perfect storm for a data protection disaster.

The real cause of concern is the fact that Big Data contains all of the things you don't want to see when you are trying to protect data. Big Data can contain very unique sample sets—for example, data from devices that monitor physical elements (e.g., traffic, movement, soil pH, rain, wind) on a frequent schedule, surveillance cameras, or any other type of data that are accumulated frequently and in real time. All of the data are unique to the moment, and if they are lost, they are impossible to recreate.

That uniqueness also means you cannot leverage time-saving backup preparation and security technologies, such as deduplication; this greatly increases the capacity requirements for backup subsystems, slows down security scanning, makes it harder to detect data corruption, and complicates archiving.

There is also the issue of the large size and number of files often found in Big Data analytic environments. In order for a backup application and associated appliances or hardware to churn through a large number of files, bandwidth to the backup systems and/or the backup appliance must be large, and the receiving devices must be able to ingest data at the rate that the data can be delivered, which means that significant CPU processing power is necessary to churn through billions of files.

There is more to backup than just processing files. Big Data normally includes a database component, which cannot be overlooked. Analytic information is often processed into an Oracle, NoSQL, or Hadoop environment of some type, so real-time (or live) protection of that environment may be required. A database component shifts the backup ideology from a massive number of small files to be backed up to a small number of massive files to be backed up. That changes the dynamics of how backups need to be processed.

Big Data often presents the worst-case scenario for most backup appliances, in which the workload mix consists of billions of small files and a small number of large files. Finding a backup solution that can ingest this mixed workload of data at full speed and that can scale to massive capacities may be the biggest challenge in the Big Data backup market.

BIG DATA AND COMPLIANCE

Compliance issues are becoming a big concern in the data center, and these issues have a major effect on how Big Data is protected, stored, accessed, and archived. Whether Big Data is going to reside in the data warehouse or in some other more scalable data store remains unresolved for most of the industry; it is an evolving paradigm. However, one thing is certain: Big Data is not easily handled by the relational databases that the typical database administrator is used to working with in the traditional enterprise database server environment. This means it is harder to understand how compliance affects the data.

Big Data is transforming the storage and access paradigms to an emerging new world of horizontally scaling, unstructured databases, which are better at solving some old business problems through analytics. More important, this new world of file types and data is prompting analysis professionals to think of new problems to solve, some of which have never been attempted before. With that in mind, it becomes easy to see that a rebalancing of the database landscape is about to commence, and data architects will finally embrace the fact that relational databases are no longer the only tool in the tool kit.

This has everything to do with compliance. New data types and methodologies are still expected to meet the legislative requirements placed on businesses by compliance laws. There will be no excuses accepted and no passes given if a new data methodology breaks the law.

Preventing compliance from becoming the next Big Data nightmare is going to be the job of security professionals. They will have to ask themselves some important questions and take into account the growing mass of data, which are becoming increasingly unstructured and are accessed from a distributed cloud of users and applications looking to slice and dice them in a million and one ways. How will security professionals be sure they are keeping tabs on the regulated information in all that mix?

Many organizations still have to grasp the importance of such areas as payment card industry and personal health information compliance and are failing to take the necessary steps because the Big Data elements are moving through the enterprise with other basic data. The trend seems to be that as businesses jump into Big Data, they forget to worry about very specific pieces of information that may be mixed into their large data stores, exposing them to compliance issues.

Health care probably provides the best example for those charged with compliance as they examine how Big Data creation, storage, and flow work in their organizations. The move to electronic health record systems, driven by the Health Insurance Portability and Accountability Act (HIPAA) and other legislation, is causing a dramatic increase in the accumulation, access, and inter-enterprise exchange of personal identifying information. That has already created a Big Data problem for the largest health care providers and payers, and it must be solved to maintain compliance.

The concepts of Big Data are as applicable to health care as they are to other businesses. The types of data are as varied and vast as the devices collecting the data, and while the concept of collecting and analyzing the unstructured data is not new, recently developed technologies make it quicker and easier than ever to store, analyze, and manipulate these massive data sets.

Health care deals with these massive data sets using Big Data stores, which can span tens of thousands of computers to enable enterprises, researchers, and governments to develop innovative products, make important discoveries, and generate new revenue streams. The rapid evolution of Big Data has forced vendors and architects to focus primarily on the storage, performance, and availability elements, while security—which is often thought to diminish performance—has largely been an afterthought.

In the medical industry, the primary problem is that unsecured Big Data stores are filled with content that is collected and analyzed in real time and is often extraordinarily sensitive: intellectual property, personal identifying information, and other confidential information. The disclosure of this type of data, by either attack or human error, can be devastating to a company and its reputation.

However, because this unstructured Big Data doesn't fit into traditional, structured, SQL-based relational databases, NoSQL, a new type of data management approach, has evolved. These nonrelational data stores can store, manage, and manipulate terabytes, petabytes, and even exabytes of data in real time.

No longer scattered in multiple federated databases throughout the enterprise, Big Data consolidates information in a single massive database stored in distributed clusters and can be easily deployed in the cloud to save costs and ease management. Companies may also move Big Data to the cloud for disaster recovery, replication, load balancing, storage, and other purposes.

Unfortunately, most of the data stores in use today—including Hadoop, Cassandra, and MongoDB—do not incorporate sufficient data security tools to provide enterprises with the peace of mind that confidential data will remain safe and secure at all times. The need for security and privacy of enterprise data is not a new concept. However, the development of Big Data changes the situation in many ways. To date, those charged with network security have spent a great deal of time and money on perimeter-based security mechanisms such as firewalls, but perimeter enforcement cannot prevent unauthorized access to data once a criminal or a hacker has entered the network.

Add to this the fact that most Big Data platforms provide little to no data-level security along with the alarming truth that Big Data centralizes most critical, sensitive, and proprietary data in a single logical data store, and it's clear that Big Data requires big security.

The lessons learned by the health care industry show that there is a way to keep Big Data secure and in compliance. A combination of technologies has been assembled to meet four important goals:

1. **Control access by process, not job function.** Server and network administrators, cloud administrators, and other employees often have access to more information than their jobs require because the systems simply lack the appropriate access controls. Just because a user has operating system–level access to a specific server does not mean that he or she needs, or should have, access to the Big Data stored on that server.

2. **Secure the data at rest.** Most consumers today would not conduct an online transaction without seeing the familiar padlock

symbol or at least a certification notice designating that particular transaction as encrypted and secure. So why wouldn't you require the same data to be protected at rest in a Big Data store? All Big Data, especially sensitive information, should remain encrypted, whether it is stored on a disk, on a server, or in the cloud and regardless of whether the cloud is inside or outside the walls of your organization.

3. **Protect the cryptographic keys and store them separately from the data.** Cryptographic keys are the gateway to the encrypted data. If the keys are left unprotected, the data are easily compromised. Organizations—often those that have cobbled together their own encryption and key management solution—will sometimes leave the key exposed within the configuration file or on the very server that stores the encrypted data. This leads to the frightening reality that any user with access to the server, authorized or not, can access the key and the data. In addition, that key may be used for any number of other servers. Storing the cryptographic keys on a separate, hardened server, either on the premises or in the cloud, is the best practice for keeping data safe and an important step in regulatory compliance. The bottom line is to treat key security with as much, if not greater, rigor than the data set itself.

4. **Create trusted applications and stacks to protect data from rogue users.** You may encrypt your data to control access, but what about the user who has access to the config-uration files that define the access controls to those data? Encrypting more than just the data and hardening the security of your overall environment—including applications, services, and configurations—gives you peace of mind that your sensi-tive information is protected from malicious users and rogue employees.

There is still time to create and deploy appropriate security rules and compliance objectives. The health care industry has helped to lay some of the groundwork. However, the slow development of laws and regulations works in favor of those trying to get ahead on Big Data. Currently, many of the laws and regulations have not addressed the unique challenges of data warehousing. Many of the regulations do not address the rules for protecting data from different customers at different levels.

For example, if a database has credit card data and health care data, do the PCI Security Standards Council and HIPAA apply to the entire data store or only to the parts of the data store that have their types of data? The answer is highly dependent on your interpretation of the requirements and the way you have implemented the technology.

Similarly, social media applications that are collecting tons of unregulated yet potentially sensitive data may not yet be a compliance concern. But they are still a security problem that if not properly addressed now may be regulated in the future. Social networks are accumulating massive amounts of unstructured data—a primary fuel for Big Data, but they are not yet regulated, so this is not a compliance concern but remains as a security concern.

Security professionals concerned about how things like Hadoop and NoSQL deployments are going to affect their compliance efforts should take a deep breath and remember that the general principles of data security still apply. The first principle is knowing where the data reside. With the newer database solutions, there are automated ways of detecting data and triaging systems that appear to have data they shouldn't.

Once you begin to map and understand the data, opportunities should become evident that will lead to automating and monitoring compliance and security through data warehouse technologies. Automation offers the ability to decrease compliance and security costs and still provide the higher levels of assurance, which validates where the data are and where they are going.

Of course, automation does not solve every problem for security, compliance, and backup. There are still some very basic rules that should be used to enable security while not derailing the value of Big Data:

- **Ensure that security does not impede performance or availability.** Big Data is all about handling volume while providing results, being able to deal with the velocity and variety of data, and allowing organizations to capture, analyze, store, or move data in real time. Security controls that limit any of these processes are a nonstarter for organizations serious about Big Data.

- **Pick the right encryption scheme.** Some data security solutions encrypt at the file level or lower, such as including specific data values, documents, or rows and columns. Those methodologies can be cumbersome, especially for key management. File level or internal file encryption can also render data unusable because many applications cannot analyze encrypted data. Likewise, encryption at the operating system level, but without advanced key management and process-based access controls, can leave Big Data woefully insecure. To maintain the high levels of performance required to analyze Big Data, consider a transparent data encryption solution optimized for Big Data.

- **Ensure that the security solution can evolve with your changing requirements.** Vendor lock-in is becoming a major concern for many enterprises. Organizations do not want to be held captive to a sole source for security, whether it is a single-server vendor, a network vendor, a cloud provider, or a platform. The flexibility to migrate between cloud providers and models based on changing business needs is a requirement, and this is no different with Big Data technologies. When evaluating security, you should consider a solution that is platform-agnostic and can work with any Big Data file system or database, including Hadoop, Cassandra, and MongoDB.

THE INTELLECTUAL PROPERTY CHALLENGE

One of the biggest issues around Big Data is the concept of intellectual property (IP). First we must understand what IP is, in its most basic form. There are many definitions available, but basically, intellectual property refers to creations of the human mind, such as inventions, literary and artistic works, and symbols, names, images, and designs used in commerce. Although this is a rather broad description, it conveys the essence of IP.

With Big Data consolidating all sorts of private, public, corporate, and government data into a large data store, there are bound to be pieces of IP in the mix: simple elements, such as photographs, to more complex elements, such as patent applications or engineering diagrams. That information has to be properly protected, which may prove to be difficult, since Big Data analytics is designed to find nuggets of information and report on them.

Here is a little background: Between 1985 and 2010, the number of patents granted worldwide rose from slightly less than 400,000 to more than 900,000. That's an increase of more than 125 percent over one generation (25 years). Patents are filed and backed with IP rights (IPRs).

Technology is obviously pushing this growth forward, so it only makes sense that Big Data will be used to look at IP and IP rights to determine opportunity. This should create a major concern for companies looking to protect IP and should also be a catalyst to take action. Fortunately, protecting IP in the realm of Big Data follows many of the same rules that organizations have already come to embrace, so IP protection should already be part of the culture in any enterprise.

The same concepts just have to be expanded into the realm of Big Data. Some basic rules are as follows:

- **Understand what IP is and know what you have to protect.** If all employees understand what needs to be protected, they can better understand how to protect it and whom to protect it from. Doing that requires that those charged with IP security in IT (usually a computer security officer, or CSO) must communicate on an ongoing basis with the executives who oversee intellectual capital. This may require meeting at least quarterly with the chief executive, operating, and information officers and representatives from HR, marketing, sales, legal services, production, and research and development (R&D). Corporate leaders will be the foundation for protecting IP.

- **Prioritize protection.** CSOs with extensive experience normally recommend doing a risk and cost-benefit analysis. This may require you to create a map of your company's assets and determine what information, if lost, would hurt your company the most. Then consider which of those assets are most at risk of being stolen. Putting these two factors together should help you figure out where to best allocate your protective efforts.

- **Label.** Confidential information should be labeled appropriately. If company data are proprietary, note that on every log-in screen. This may sound trivial, but in court you may have to prove that someone who was not authorized to take information had been informed repeatedly. Your argument won't stand up if you can't demonstrate that you made this clear.

- **Lock it up.** Physical as well as digital protection schemes are a must. Rooms that store sensitive data should be locked. This applies to everything from the server farm to the file room. Keep track of who has the keys, always use complex passwords, and limit employee access to important databases.

- **Educate employees.** Awareness training can be effective for plugging and preventing IP leaks, but it must be targeted to the information that a specific group of employees needs to guard. Talk in specific terms about something that engineers or scientists have invested a lot of time in, and they will pay attention. Humans are often the weakest link in the defense chain. This is why an IP protection effort that counts on firewalls and copyrights but ignores employee awareness and training is doomed to fail.

- **Know your tools.** A growing variety of software tools are available for tracking documents and other IP stores. The category of data loss protection (or data leakage prevention) grew quickly in the middle of the first decade of this century and now shows signs of consolidation into other security tool sets. Those tools can locate sensitive documents and keep track of how they are being used and by whom.

- **Use a holistic approach.** You must take a panoramic view of security. If someone is scanning the internal network, your internal intrusion detection system goes off, and someone from IT calls the employee who is doing the scanning and says, "Stop doing that." The employee offers a plausible explanation, and that's the end of it. Later the night watchman sees an employee carrying out protected documents, whose explanation, when stopped, is "Oops, I didn't realize that got into my briefcase." Over time, the HR group, the audit group, the individual's colleagues, and others all notice isolated incidents, but no one puts them together and realizes that all these breaches were perpetrated by the same person. This is why communication gaps between infosecurity and corporate security groups can be so harmful. IP protection requires connections and communication among all the corporate functions. The legal department has to play a role in IP protection, and so does HR, IT, R&D, engineering, and graphic design. Think holistically, both to protect and to detect.

- **Use a counterintelligence mind-set.** If you were spying on your own company, how would you do it? Thinking through such tactics will lead you to consider protecting phone lists, shredding the papers in the recycling bins, convening an internal council to approve your R&D scientists' publications, and coming up with other worthwhile ideas for your particular business.

These guidelines can be applied to almost any information security paradigm that is geared toward protecting IP. The same guidelines can be used when designing IP protection for a Big Data platform.

CHAPTER **8**

The Evolution of Big Data

To truly understand the implications of Big Data analytics, one has to reach back into the annals of computing history, specifically business intelligence (BI) and scientific computing. The ideology behind Big Data can most likely be tracked back to the days before the age of computers, when unstructured data were the norm (paper records) and analytics was in its infancy. Perhaps the first Big Data challenge came in the form of the 1880 U.S. census, when the information concerning approximately 50 million people had to be gathered, classified, and reported on.

With the 1880 census, just counting people was not enough information for the U.S. government to work with—particular elements, such as age, sex, occupation, education level, and even the "number of insane people in household," had to be accounted for. That information had intrinsic value to the process, but only if it could be tallied, tabulated, analyzed, and presented. New methods of relating the data to other data collected came into being, such as associating occupations with geographic areas, birth rates with education levels, and countries of origin with skill sets.

The 1880 census truly yielded a mountain of data to deal with, yet only severely limited technology was available to do any of the analytics. The problem of Big Data could not be solved for the 1880 census, so it took over seven years to manually tabulate and report on the data.

With the 1890 census, things began to change, thanks to the introduction of the first Big Data platform: a mechanical device called the Hollerith Tabulating System, which worked with punch cards that could hold about 80 variables. The Hollerith Tabulating System revolutionized the value of census data, making it actionable and increasing its value an untold amount. Analysis now took six weeks instead of seven years. That allowed the government to act on information in a reasonable amount of time.

The census example points out a common theme with data analytics: Value can be derived only by analyzing data in a time frame in which action can still be taken to utilize the information uncovered. For the U.S. government, the ability to analyze the 1890 census led to an improved understanding of the populace, which the government could use to shape economic and social policies ranging from taxation to education to military conscription.

In today's world, the information contained in the 1890 census would no longer be considered Big Data, according to the definition: data sets so large that common technology cannot accommodate and process them. Today's desktop computers certainly have enough horsepower to process the information contained in the 1890 census by using a simple relational database and some basic code.

That realization transforms what Big Data is all about. Big Data involves having more data than you can handle with the computing power you already have, and you cannot easily scale your current computing environment to address the data. The definition of Big Data therefore continues to evolve with time and advances in technology. Big Data will always remain a paradigm shift in the making.

That said, the momentum behind Big Data continues to be driven by the realization that large unstructured data sources, such as those from the 1890 census, can deliver almost immeasurable value. The next giant leap for Big Data analytics came with the Manhattan Project, the U.S. development of the atomic bomb during World War II. The Manhattan Project not only introduced the concept of Big Data analysis with computers, it was also the catalyst for "Big Science," which in turn depends on Big Data analytics for success. The next largest Big Science project began in the late 1950s with the launch of the U.S. space program.

As the term *Big Science* gained currency in the 1960s, the Manhattan Project and the space program became paradigmatic examples. However, the International Geophysical Year, an international scientific project that lasted from July 1, 1957, to December 31, 1958, provided scientists with an alternative model: a synoptic collection of observational data on a global scale.

This new, potentially complementary model of Big Science encompassed multiple fields of practice and relied heavily on the sharing of large data sets that spanned multiple disciplines. The change in data gathering techniques, analysis, and collaboration also helped to redefine how Big Science projects are planned and accomplished. Most important, the International Geophysical Year project laid the foundation for more ambitious projects that gathered more specialized data for specific analysis, such as the International Biological Program and later the Long-Term Ecological Research Network. Both increased the mountains of data gathered, incorporated newer analysis technologies, and pushed IT technology further into the spotlight.

The International Biological Program encountered difficulties when the institutional structures, research methodologies, and data management implied by the Big Science mode of research collided with the epistemic goals, practices, and assumptions of many of the scientists involved. By 1974, when the program ended, many participants viewed it as a failure.

Nevertheless, what many viewed as a failure really was a success. The program transformed the way data were collected, shared, and analyzed and redefined how IT can be used for data analysis. Historical analysis suggests that many of the original incentives of the program (such as the emphasis on Big Data and the implementation of the organizational structure of Big Science) were in fact realized by the program's visionaries and its immediate investigators. Even though the program failed to follow the exact model of the International Geophysical Year, it ultimately succeeded in providing a renewed legitimacy for synoptic data collection.

The lessons learned from the birth of Big Science spawned new Big Data projects: weather prediction, physics research (supercollider data analytics), astronomy images (planet detection), medical research (drug interaction), and many others. Of course, Big Data doesn't apply only to science; businesses have latched onto its techniques, methodologies, and objectives, too. This has allowed the businesses to uncover value in data that might previously have been overlooked.

BIG DATA: THE MODERN ERA

Big Science may have led to the birth of Big Data, but it was Big Business that brought Big Data through its adolescence into the modern era. Big Science and Big Business differ on many levels, of course, especially in analytics. Big Science uses Big Data to answer questions or prove theories, while Big Business uses Big Data to discover new opportunities, measure efficiencies, or uncover relationships among what was thought to be unrelated data sets.

Nonetheless, both use algorithms to mine data, and both have to have technologies to work with mountains of data. But the similarities end there. Big Science gathers data based on experiments and research conducted in controlled environments. Big Business gathers data from sources that are transactional in nature and that often have little control over the origin of the data.

For Big Business, and businesses of almost any size, there is an avalanche of data available that is increasing exponentially. Perhaps Google CEO Erik Schmidt said it best: "Every two days now we create as much information as we did from the dawn of civilization up until 2003. That's something like five exabytes of data." An exabyte is an incredibly large, almost unimaginable amount of information: 10 to the 18th power. Think of an exabyte as the number 1 followed by 18 zeros.

It is that massive amount of exponentially growing data that defines the future of Big Data. Once again, we may need to look at the scientific community to determine where Big Data is headed for the business world. Farnam Jahanian, the assistant director for computer and information science and engineering for the National Science Foundation (NSF), kicked off a May 1, 2012, briefing about Big Data on Capitol Hill by calling data "a transformative new currency for science, engineering, education, and commerce." That briefing, which was organized by TechAmerica, brought together a panel of leaders from government and industry to discuss the opportunities for innovation arising from the collection, storage, analysis, and visualization of large, heterogeneous data sets, all the while taking into consideration the significant security and privacy implications.

Jahanian noted that "Big Data is characterized not only by the enormous volume of data but also by the diversity and heterogeneity of the data and the velocity of its generation," the result of modern experimental methods, longitudinal observational studies, scientific instruments such as telescopes and particle accelerators, Internet transactions, and the widespread deployment of sensors all around us. In doing so, he set the stage for why Big Data is important to all facets of the IT discovery and innovation ecosystem, including the nation's academic, government, industrial, entrepreneurial, and investment communities.

Jahanian further explained the implications of the modern era of Big Data with three specific points:

> First, insights and more accurate predictions from large and complex collections of data have important implications for the economy. Access to information is transforming traditional businesses and is creating opportunities in new markets. Big Data is driving the creation of new IT products and services based on business intelligence and data analytics and is boosting the productivity of firms that use it to make better decisions and identify new business trends.
>
> Second, advances in Big Data are critical to accelerate the pace of discovery in almost every science and engineering discipline. From new insights about protein structure, biomedical research and clinical decision making, and climate modeling to new ways to mitigate and respond to natural disasters and new strategies for effective learning and education, there are enormous opportunities for data-driven discovery.
>
> Third, Big Data also has the potential to solve some of the nation's most pressing challenges—in science, education, environment and sustainability, medicine, commerce, and cyber and national security—with enormous societal benefit and laying the foundations for U.S. competitiveness for many decades to come.

Jahanian shared the President's Council of Advisors on Science and Technology's recent recommendation for the federal government to "increase R&D investments for collecting, storing, preserving, managing, analyzing, and sharing increased quantities of data," because "the potential to gain new insights [by moving] from data to knowledge to action has tremendous potential to transform all areas of national priority."

Partly in response to this recommendation, the White House Office of Science and Technology Policy, together with other agencies, announced a $200 million Big Data R&D initiative to advance core techniques and technologies. According to Jahanian, within this initiative, the NSF's strategy for supporting the fundamental science and underlying infrastructure enabling Big Data science and engineering involves the following:

- Advances in foundational techniques and technologies (i.e., new methods) to derive knowledge from data.
- Cyberinfrastructure to manage, curate, and serve data to science and engineering research and education communities.
- New approaches to education and workforce development.
- Nurturance of new types of collaborations—multidisciplinary teams and communities enabled by new data access policies—to make advances in the grand challenges of the computation- and data-intensive world today.

Ultimately, Jahanian concluded, "realizing the enormous potential of Big Data requires a long-term, bold, sustainable, and comprehensive approach, not only by NSF but also throughout the government and our nation's research institutions."

The panel discussions that followed echoed many of Jahanian's remarks. For example, Nuala O'Connor Kelly, the senior counsel for information governance and chief privacy leader at General Electric (GE), said, "For us, it's the volume and velocity and variety of data [and the opportunity that's presented for using] that data to achieve new results for the company and for our customers and clients [throughout the world]." She cited as an example that GE Healthcare collects and monitors maintenance data from its machines deployed worldwide and can automatically ship replacement parts just days in advance of their malfunctioning, based on the analytics of machine functionality. "Much of [this] is done remotely and at tremendous cost savings," she said.

Caron Kogan, the strategic planning director at Lockheed Martin, and Flavio Villanustre, the vice president of technology at LexisNexis Risk Solutions, described similar pursuits within their companies— particularly in intelligence and fraud prevention, respectively.

GE's Kelly touched on privacy aspects. "Control may no longer be about not having the data at all," she pointed out. "A potentially more efficient solution is one of making sure there are appropriate controls technologically and processes and policies and laws in place and then ensuring appropriate enforcement." She emphasized striking the right balance between policies that ensure the protection of individuals and those that enable technological innovation and economic growth.

Bill Perlowitz, the chief technology officer in Wyle Laboratories's science, technology, and engineering group, referenced a paradigm shift in scientific exploration:

> Before, if you had an application or software, you had
> value; now that value is going to be in the data. For
> scientists that represents a shift from [hypothesis-driven]
> science to data-driven research. Hypothesis-driven science
> limits your exploration to what you can imagine, and
> the human mind . . . can only go so far. Data-driven
> science allows us to collect data and then see what it tells us,
> and we don't have a pretense that we may understand
> what those relationships are and what we may find. So for
> a research scientist, these kinds of changes are very
> exciting and something we've been trying to get to for some
> time now.

Perhaps Nick Combs, the federal chief technology officer at EMC Corporation, summed it up best when describing the unprecedented growth in data: "It's [no longer about finding a] needle in a haystack or connecting the dots. That's child's play."

What all of this means is that the value of Big Data and the transformation of the ideologies and technologies are already here. The government and scientific communities are preparing themselves for the next evolution of Big Data and are planning how to address the new challenges and figure out better ways to leverage the data.

TODAY, TOMORROW, AND THE NEXT DAY

As the amount of data gathered grows exponentially, so does the evolution of the technology used to process the data. According to the International Data Corporation, the volume of digital content in the world will grow to 2.7 billion terabytes in 2012, up 48 percent from 2011, and will reach 8 billion terabytes by 2015. That will be a lot of data!

The flood of data is coming from both structured corporate databases and unstructured data from Web pages, blogs, social networking messages, and other sources. Currently, for example, there are countless digital sensors worldwide in industrial equipment, automobiles, electrical meters, and shipping crates. Those sensors can measure and communicate location, movement, vibration, temperature, humidity, and even chemical changes in the air. Today, Big Business wields data like a weapon. Giant retailers, such as Walmart and Kohl's, analyze sales, pricing, economic, demographic, and weather data to tailor product selections at particular stores and determine the timing of price markdowns.

Logistics companies like United Parcel Service mine data on truck delivery times and traffic patterns to fine-tune routing. A whole ecosystem of new businesses and technologies is springing up to engage with this new reality: companies that store data, companies that mine data for insight, and companies that aggregate data to make them manageable. However, it is an ecosystem that is still emerging, and its exact shape has yet to make itself clear.

Even though Big Data has been around for some time, one of the biggest challenges of working with it still remains, and that is assembling data and preparing them for analysis. Different systems store data in different formats, even within the same company. Assembling, standardizing, and cleaning data of irregularities—all without removing the information that makes them valuable—remain a central challenge.

Currently, Hadoop, an open source software framework derived from Google's MapReduce and Google File System papers, is being used by several technology vendors to do just that. Hadoop maps tasks across a cluster of machines, splitting them into smaller subtasks, before reducing the results into one master calculation. It's really an old grid-computing technique given new life in the age of cloud computing. Many of the challenges of yesterday remain today, and technology is just now catching up with the demands of Big Data analytics. However, Big Data remains a moving target.

As the future brings more challenges, it will also deliver more solutions, and Big Data has a bright future, with tomorrow delivering the technologies that ease leveraging the data. For example, Hadoop is converging with other technology advances such as high-speed data analysis, made possible by parallel computing, in-memory processing, and lower-cost flash memory in the form of solid-state drives.

The prospect of being able to process troves of data very quickly, in-memory, without time-consuming forays to retrieve information stored on disk drives, will be a major enabler, and this will allow companies to assemble, sort, and analyze data much more rapidly. For example, T-Mobile is using SAP's HANA to mine data on its 30 million U.S. customers from stores, text messages, and call centers to tailor personalized deals.

What used to take T-Mobile a week to accomplish can now be done in three hours with the SAP system. Organizations that can utilize this capability to make faster and more informed business decisions will have a distinct advantage over competitors. In a short period of time, Hadoop has transitioned from relative obscurity as a consumer Internet project into the mainstream consciousness of enterprise IT.

Hadoop is designed to handle mountains of unstructured data. However, as it exists, the open source code is a long way from meeting enterprise requirements for security, management, and efficiency without some serious customization. Enterprise-scale Hadoop deployments require costly IT specialists who are capable of guiding a lot of somewhat disjointed processes. That currently limits adoption to organizations with substantial IT budgets.

As tomorrow delivers refined platforms, Hadoop and its derivatives will start to fit into the enterprise as a complement to existing data analytics and data warehousing tools, available from established business process vendors, such as Oracle, HP, and SAP. The key will be to make Hadoop much more accessible to enterprises of all sizes, which can be accomplished by creating high availability platforms that take much of the complexity out of assembling and preparing huge amounts of data for analysis.

Aggregating multiple steps into a streamlined automated process with significantly enhanced security will prove to be the catalyst that drives Big Data from today to tomorrow. Add those enhancements to new technologies, such as appliances, and the momentum should continue to pick up, thanks to easy management through user-friendly GUI.

The true value of Big Data lies in the amount of useful data that can be derived from it. The future of Big Data is therefore to do for data and analytics what Moore's Law has done for computing hardware and exponentially increase the speed and value of business intelligence. Whether the need is to link geography and retail availability, use patient data to forecast public health trends, or analyze global climate trends, we live in a world full of data. Effectively harnessing Big Data will give businesses a whole new lens through which to see it.

However, the advance of Big Data technology doesn't stop with tomorrow. Beyond tomorrow probably holds surprises that no one has even imagined yet. As technology marches ahead, so will the usefulness of Big Data. A case in point is IBM's Watson, an artificial intelligence computer system capable of answering questions posed in natural language. In 2011, as a test of its abilities, Watson competed on the quiz show *Jeopardy!*, in the show's only human-versus-machine match to date. In a two-game, combined-point match, broadcast in three episodes aired February 14–16, Watson beat Brad Rutter, the biggest all-time money winner on *Jeopardy!*, and Ken Jennings, the record holder for the longest championship streak (74 wins).

Watson had access to 200 million pages of structured and unstructured content consuming four terabytes of disk storage, including the full text of Wikipedia, but was not connected to the Internet during the game. Watson demonstrated that there are new ways to deal with Big Data and new ways to measure results, perhaps exemplifying where Big Data may be headed.

So what's next for Watson? IBM has stated publicly that Watson was a client-driven initiative, and the company intends to push Watson in directions that best serve customer needs. IBM is now working with financial giant Citi to explore how the Watson technology could improve and simplify the banking experience. Watson's applicability doesn't end with banking, however; IBM has also teamed up with health insurer WellPoint to turn Watson into a machine that can support the doctors of the world.

According to IBM, Watson is best suited for use cases involving critical decision making based on large volumes of unstructured data. To drive the Big Data–crunching message home, IBM has stated that 90 percent of the world's data was created in the last two years, and 80 percent of that data is unstructured. Furthering the value proposition of Watson and Big Data, IBM has also stated that five new research documents come out of Wall Street every minute, and medical information is doubling every five years.

IBM views the future of Big Data a little differently than other vendors do, most likely based on its Watson research. In IBM's future, Watson becomes a service—as IBM calls it, Watson-as-a-Service—which will be delivered as a private or hybrid cloud service.

Watson aside, the health care industry seems ripe as a source of prediction for how Big Data will evolve. Examples abound for the benefits of Big Data and the medical field; however, getting there is another story altogether. Health care (or in this context, "Big Medicine") has some specific challenges to overcome and some specific goals to achieve to realize the potential of Big Data:

- Big Medicine is drowning in information while also dying of thirst. For those in the medical profession, that axiom can be summed up with a situation that most medical personnel face: When you're in the institution and you're trying to figure out what's going on and how to report on something, you're dying of thirst in a sea of information. There is a tremendous amount of information, so much so that it becomes a Big Data problem. How does one tap into that information and make sense of it? The answer has implications not only for patients but also for the service providers, ranging from nurses, physicians, and hospital administrators, even to government and insurance agencies. The big issue is that the data are not organized; they are a mixture of structured and unstructured data. How the data will ultimately be handled over the next few years will be driven by the government, which will require a tremendous amount of information to be recorded for reporting purposes.

▪ Technologies that tap into Big Data need to become more prevalent and even ubiquitous. From the patient's perspective, analytics and Big Data will aid in determining which hospital in a patient's immediate area is the best for treating his or her condition. Today there are a huge number of choices available, and most people choose by word of mouth, insurance requirements, doctor recommendations, and many other factors. Wouldn't it make more sense to pick a facility based on report cards derived by analytics? That is the goal of the government, which wants patients to be able to look at a report card for various institutions. However, the only way to create that report card is to unlock all of the information and impose regulations and reporting. That will require various types of IT to tap into unstructured information, like dashboard technologies and analytics, business intelligence technologies, clinical intelligence technologies, and revenue cycle management intelligence for institutions.

▪ Decision support needs to be easier to access. Currently in medical institutions, evidence-based medicine and decision support is not as easy to access as it should be. Utilizing Big Data analytics will make the decision process easier and will provide the hard evidence to validate a particular decision path. For example, when a patient is suffering from a particular condition, there's a high potential that something is going to happen to that patient because of his or her history. The likely outcomes or progressions can be brought up at the beginning of the care cycle, and the treating physician can be informed immediately. Information like that and much more will come from the Big Data analytics process.

▪ Information needs to flow more easily. Currently from a patient's perspective, health care today limits information. Patients often have little perspective on what exactly is happening, at least until a physician comes in. However, the majority of patients are apprehensive about talking to the physician. That becomes an informational blockade for both the physician and the patient and creates a situation in which it becomes more difficult for both physicians and patients to make choices. Big Data has the potential to solve that problem as well; the flow of information will be easier not only for physicians to manage but also for patients to access. For example, physicians will be able to look on their tablets or smartphones and see there is a 15-minute emergency-room wait over here and a 5-minute wait over there. Scheduling, diagnostic support, and evidence-based medicine support in the work flow will improve.

- Quality of care needs to be increased while driving costs down. From a cost perspective and a quality-of-care point of view, there are a number of different areas that can be improved by Big Data. For example, if a patient experiences an injury while staying in a hospital, the hospital will not be reimbursed for his or her care. The system can see that this has the potential to happen and can alert everyone. Big Data can enable a proactive approach for care that reduces accidents or other problems that affect the quality of care. By preventing problems and accidents, Big Data can yield significant savings.

- The physician–patient relationship needs to improve. Thanks to social media and mobile applications, which are benefiting from Big Data techniques, it is becoming easier to research health issues and allow patients and physicians to communicate more frequently. Stored data and unstructured data can be analyzed against social data to identify health trends. That information can then be used by hospitals to keep patients healthier and out of the facility. In the past, hospitals made more money the sicker a patient was and the longer they kept him or her there. However, with health care reform, hospitals are going to start being compensated for keeping patients healthier. Because of that there will be an explosion of mobile applications and even social media, allowing patients to have easier access to nurses and physicians. Health care is undergoing a transformation in which the focus is more on keeping patients healthy and driving down costs. These two major areas are going to drive a great deal of change, and a lot of evolution will take place from a health information technology point of view, all underpinned by the availability of data.

Health care proves that Big Data has definite value and will arguably be the leader in Big Data developments. However, the lessons learned by the health care industry can readily be applied to other business models, because Big Data is all about knowing how to utilize and analyze data to fit specific needs.

CHANGING ALGORITHMS

Just as data evolve and force the evolution of Big Data platforms, the very basic elements of analytics evolve as well. Most approaches to dealing with large data sets within a classification learning paradigm attempt to increase computational efficiency. Given the same amount of time, a more efficient algorithm can explore more of the hypothesis space than a less efficient algorithm. If the hypothesis space contains an optimal solution, a more efficient algorithm has a greater chance of finding that solution (assuming the hypothesis space cannot be exhaustively searched within a reasonable time). It is that desire for efficiency and speed that is forcing the evolution of algorithms and the supporting systems that run them.

However, a more efficient algorithm results in more searching or a faster search, not a better search. If the learning biases of the algorithm are inappropriate, an increase in computational efficiency may not equal an improvement in prediction performance. Therein lies the problem: More efficient algorithms normally do not lead to additional insights, just improved performance. However, improving the performance of a Big Data analytics platform increases the amount of data that can be analyzed, and that may lead to new insights.

The trick here is to create new algorithms that are more flexible, that incorporate machine learning techniques, and that remove the bias from analysis. Computer systems are now becoming powerful and subtle enough to help reduce human biases from our decision making. And this is the key: Computers can do it in real time. That will inevitably transform the objective observer concept into an organic, evolving database.

Today these systems can chew through billions of bits of data, analyze them via self-learning algorithms, and package the insights for immediate use. Neither we nor the computers are perfect, but in tandem we might neutralize our biased, intuitive failings when we price a car, prescribe a medicine, or deploy a sales force.

In the real world, accurate algorithms will translate to fewer hunches and more facts. Take, for example, the banking and mortgage market, where even the most knowledgeable human can quickly be outdone by an algorithm. Big Data systems are now of such scale that they can analyze the value of tens of thousands of mortgage-backed securities by picking apart the ongoing, dynamic creditworthiness of tens of millions of individual home owners. Such a system has already been built for Wall Street traders.

By crunching billions of data points about traffic flows, an algorithm might find that on Fridays a delivery fleet should stick to the highways, despite the gut instinct of a dispatcher for surface road shortcuts.

Big Data is at an evolutionary juncture where human judgment can be improved or even replaced by machines. That may sound ominous, but the same systems are already predicting hurricanes, warning of earthquakes, and mapping tornadoes.

Businesses are seeing the value, and the systems and algorithms are starting to supplement human judgment and are even on a path to replace it, in some cases. Until recently, however, businesses have been thwarted by the cost of storage, slower processing speeds, and the flood of the data themselves, spread sloppily across scores of different databases inside one company.

With technology and pricing points now solving those problems, the evolution of algorithms and Big Data platforms is bound to accelerate and change the very way we do predictive analysis, research, and even business.

CHAPTER **9**

Best Practices for
Big Data Analytics

L ike any other technology or process, there obviously are best practices that can be applied to the problems of Big Data. In most cases, best practices usually arise from years of testing and measuring results, giving them a solid foundation to build on. However, Big Data, as it is applied today, is relatively new, short circuiting the tried-and-true methodology used in the past to derive best practices. Nevertheless, best practices are presenting themselves at a fairly accelerated rate, which means that we can still learn from the mistakes and successes of others to define what works best and what doesn't.

The evolutionary aspect of Big Data tends to affect best practices, so what may be best today may not necessarily be best tomorrow. That said, there are still some core proven techniques that can be applied to Big Data analytics and that should withstand the test of time. With new terms, new skill sets, new products, and new providers, the world of Big Data analytics can seem unfamiliar, but tried-and-true data management best practices do hold up well in this still emerging discipline.

As with any business intelligence (BI) and/or data warehouse initiative, it is critical to have a clear understanding of an organization's data management requirements and a well-defined strategy before venturing too far down the Big Data analytics path. Big Data analytics is widely hyped, and companies in all sectors are being flooded with new data sources and ever larger amounts of information. Yet making a big investment to attack the Big Data problem without first figuring out how doing so can really add value to the business is one of the most serious missteps for would-be users.

The trick is to start from a business perspective and not get too hung up on the technology, which may entail mediating conversations among the chief information officer (CIO), the data scientists, and other businesspeople to identify what the business objectives are and what value can be derived. Defining exactly what data are available and mapping out how an organization can best leverage the resources is a key part of that exercise.

CIOs, IT managers, and BI and data warehouse professionals need to examine what data are being retained, aggregated, and utilized and compare that with what data are being thrown away. It is also critical to consider external data sources that are currently not being tapped but that could be a compelling addition to the mix. Even if companies aren't sure how and when they plan to jump into Big Data analytics, there are benefits to going through this kind of an evaluation sooner rather than later.

Beginning the process of accumulating data also makes you better prepared for the eventual leap to Big Data, even if you don't know what you are going to use it for at the outset. The trick is to start accumulating the information as soon as possible. Otherwise there may be a missed opportunity because information may fall through the cracks, and you may not have that rich history of information to draw on when Big Data enters the picture.

START SMALL WITH BIG DATA

When analyzing Big Data, it makes sense to define small, high-value opportunities and use those as a starting point. Ideally, those smaller tasks will build the expertise needed to deal with the larger questions an organization may have for the analytics process. As companies expand the data sources and types of information they are looking to analyze, and as they start to create the all-important analytical models that can help them uncover patterns and correlations in both structured and unstructured data, they need to be vigilant about homing in on the findings that are most important to their stated business objectives.

It is critical to avoid situations in which you end up with a process that identifies news patterns and data relationships that offer little value to the business process. That creates a dead spot in an analytics matrix where patterns, though new, may not be relevant to the questions being asked.

Successful Big Data projects tend to start with very targeted goals and focus on smaller data sets. Only then can that success be built upon to create a true Big Data analytics methodology that starts small and grows after the practice has served the enterprise rather well, allowing value to be created with little upfront investment while preparing the company for the potential windfall of information that can be derived from analytics.

That can be accomplished by starting with "small bites" (i.e., taking individual data flows and migrating those into different systems for converged processing). Over time, those small bites will turn into big bites, and Big Data will be born. The ability to scale will prove important—as data collection increases, the scale of the system will need to grow to accommodate the data.

THINKING BIG

Leveraging open source Hadoop technologies and emerging packaged analytics tools makes an open source environment more familiar to business analysts trained in using SQL. Ultimately, scale will become the primary factor when mapping out a Big Data analytics road map, and business analysts will need to eschew the ways of SQL to grasp the concept of distributed platforms that run on nodes and clusters.

It is critical to consider what the buildup will look like. It can be accomplished by determining how much data will need to be gathered six months from now and calculating how many more servers may be needed to handle it. You will also have to make sure that the software is up to the task of scaling. One big mistake is to be ignorant about the potential growth of the solution and the potential popularity of the solution once it is rolled into production.

As analytics scales, data governance becomes increasingly important, a situation that is no different with Big Data than it is with any other large-scale network operation. The same can be said for information governance practices, which is just as important today with Big Data as it was yesterday with data warehousing. A critical caveat is to remember that information is a corporate asset and should be treated as such.

AVOIDING WORST PRACTICES

There are many potential reasons that Big Data analytics projects fall short of their goals and expectations, and in some cases it is better to know what *not* to do rather than knowing what to do. This leads us to the idea of identifying "worst practices," so that you can avoid making the same mistakes that others have made in the past. It is better to learn from the errors of others than to make your own. Some worst practices to look out for are the following:

- **Thinking "If we build it, they will come."** Many organizations make the mistake of assuming that simply deploying a data warehousing or BI system will solve critical business problems and deliver value. However, IT as well as BI and analytics program managers get sold on the technology hype and forget that business value is their first priority; data analysis technology is just a tool used to generate that value. Instead of blindly adopting and deploying something, Big Data analytics proponents first need to determine the business purposes that would be served by the technology in order to establish a business case—and only then choose and implement the right analytics tools for the job at hand. Without a solid understanding of business requirements, the danger is that project teams will end up creating a Big Data disk farm that really isn't worth anything to the organization, earning the teams an unwanted spot in the "data doghouse."

- **Assuming that the software will have all of the answers.** Building an analytics system, especially one involving Big Data, is complex and resource-intensive. As a result, many organizations hope the software they deploy will be a magic bullet that instantly does it all for them. People should know better, of course, but they still have hope. Software does help, sometimes dramatically. But Big Data analytics is only as good as the data being analyzed and the analytical skills of those using the tools.

- **Not understanding that you need to think differently.** Insanity is often defined as repeating a task and expecting different results, and there is some modicum of insanity in the world of analytics. People forget that trying what has worked for them in the past, even when they are confronted with a different situation, leads to failure. In the case of Big Data, some organizations assume that *big* just means more transactions and large data volumes. It may, but many Big Data analytics initiatives involve unstructured and semistructured information that needs to be managed and analyzed in fundamentally different ways than is the case with the structured data in enterprise applications and data warehouses. As a result, new methods and tools might be required to capture, cleanse, store, integrate, and access at least some of your Big Data.

- **Forgetting all of the lessons of the past.** Sometimes enterprises go to the other extreme and think that everything is different with Big Data and that they have to start from scratch. This mistake can be even more fatal to a Big Data analytics project's success than thinking that nothing is different. Just because the data you are looking to analyze are structured differently doesn't mean the fundamental laws of data management have been rewritten.

- **Not having the requisite business and analytical expertise.** A corollary to the misconception that the technology can do it all is the belief that all you need are IT staffers to implement Big Data analytics software. First, in keeping with the theme mentioned earlier of generating business value, an effective Big Data analytics program has to incorporate extensive business and industry knowledge into both the system design stage and ongoing operations. Second, many organizations underestimate the extent of the analytical skills that are needed. If Big Data analysis is only about building reports and dashboards, enterprises can probably just leverage their existing BI expertise. However, Big Data analytics typically involves more advanced processes, such as data mining and predictive analytics. That requires analytics professionals with statistical, actuarial, and other sophisticated skills, which might mean new hiring for organizations that are making their first forays into advanced analytics.

▪ **Treating the project like a science experiment.** Too often, companies measure the success of Big Data analytics programs merely by the fact that data are being collected and then analyzed. In reality, collecting and analyzing the data is just the beginning. Analytics only produces business value if it is incorporated into business processes, enabling business managers and users to act on the findings to improve organizational performance and results. To be truly effective, an analytics program also needs to include a feedback loop for communicating the success of actions taken as a result of analytical findings, followed by a refinement of the analytical models based on the business results.

▪ **Promising and trying to do too much.** Many Big Data analytics projects fall into a big trap: Proponents oversell how fast they can deploy the systems and how significant the business benefits will be. Overpromising and underdelivering is the surest way to get the business to walk away from any technology, and it often sets back the use of the particular technology within an organization for a long time—even if many other enterprises are achieving success. In addition, when you set expectations that the benefits will come easily and quickly, business executives have a tendency to underestimate the required level of involvement and commitment. And when a sufficient resource commitment isn't there, the expected benefits usually don't come easily or quickly—and the project is labeled a failure.

BABY STEPS

It is said that every journey begins with the first step, and the journey toward creating an effective Big Data analytics holds true to that axiom. However, it takes more than one step to reach a destination of success. Organizations embarking on Big Data analytics programs require a strong implementation plan to make sure that the analytics process works for them. Choosing the technology that will be used is only half the battle when preparing for a Big Data initiative. Once a company identifies the right database software and analytics tools and begins to put the technology infrastructure in place, it's ready to move to the next level and develop a real strategy for success.

The importance of effective project management processes to creating a successful Big Data analytics program also cannot be over-stated. The following tips offer advice on steps that businesses should take to help ensure a smooth deployment:

- **Decide what data to include and what to leave out.** By their very nature, Big Data analytics projects involve large data sets. But that doesn't mean that all of a company's data sources, or all of the information within a relevant data source, will need to be analyzed. Organizations need to identify the strategic data that will lead to valuable analytical insights. For instance, what combination of information can pinpoint key customer-retention factors? Or what data are required to uncover hidden patterns in stock market transactions? Focusing on a project's business goals in the planning stages can help an organization home in on the exact analytics that are required, after which it can—and should—look at the data needed to meet those business goals. In some cases, this will indeed mean including everything. In other cases, though, it means using only a subset of the Big Data on hand.

- **Build effective business rules and then work through the complexity they create.** Coping with complexity is the key aspect of most Big Data analytics initiatives. In order to get the right analytical outputs, it is essential to include business-focused data owners in the process to make sure that all of the necessary business rules are identified in advance. Once the rules are documented, technical staffers can assess how much complexity they create and the work required to turn the data inputs into relevant and valuable findings. That leads into the next phase of the implementation.

■ **Translate business rules into relevant analytics in a collaborative fashion.** Business rules are just the first step in developing effective Big Data analytics applications. Next, IT or analytics professionals need to create the analytical queries and algorithms required to generate the desired outputs. But that shouldn't be done in a vacuum. The better and more accurate that queries are in the first place, the less redevelopment will be required. Many projects require continual reiterations because of a lack of communication between the project team and business departments. Ongoing communication and collaboration lead to a much smoother analytics development process.

■ **Have a maintenance plan.** A successful Big Data analytics initiative requires ongoing attention and updates in addition to the initial development work. Regular query maintenance and keeping on top of changes in business requirements are important, but they represent only one aspect of managing an analytics program. As data volumes continue to increase and business users become more familiar with the analytics process, more questions will inevitably arise. The analytics team must be able to keep up with the additional requests in a timely fashion. Also, one of the requirements when evaluating Big Data analytics hardware and software options is assessing their ability to support iterative development processes in dynamic business environments. An analytics system will retain its value over time if it can adapt to changing requirements.

■ **Keep your users in mind—all of them.** With interest growing in self-service BI capabilities, it shouldn't be shocking that a focus on end users is a key factor in Big Data analytics programs. Having a robust IT infrastructure that can handle large data sets and both structured and unstructured information is important, of course. But so is developing a system that is usable and easy to interact with, and doing so means taking the various needs of users into account. Different types of people—from senior executives to operational workers, business analysts, and statisticians—will be accessing Big Data analytics applications in one way or another, and their adoption of the tools will help to ensure overall project success. That requires different levels of interactivity that match user expectations and the amount of experience they have with analytics tools—for instance, building dashboards and data visualizations to present findings in an easy-to-understand way to business managers and workers who aren't inclined to run their own Big Data analytics queries.

There's no one way to ensure Big Data analytics success. But following a set of frameworks and best practices, including the tips outlined here, can help organizations to keep their Big Data initiatives on track. The technical details of a Big Data installation are quite intensive and need to be looked at and considered in an in-depth manner. That isn't enough, though: Both the technical aspects and the business factors must be taken into account to make sure that organizations get the desired outcomes from their Big Data analytics investments.

THE VALUE OF ANOMALIES

There are people who believe that anomalies are something best ignored when processing Big Data, and they have created sophisticated scrubbing programs to discard what is considered an anomaly. That can be a sound practice when working with particular types of data, since anomalies can color the results. However, there are times when anomalies prove to be more valuable than the rest of the data in a particular context. The lesson to be learned is "Don't discard data without further analysis."

Take, for example, the world of high-end network security, where encryption is the norm, access is logged, and data are examined in real time. Here the ability to identify something that fits into the uncharacteristic movement of data is of the utmost importance—in other words, security problems are detected by looking at anomalies. That idea can be applied to almost any discipline, ranging from financial auditing to scientific inquiry to detecting cyber-threats, all critical services that are based on identifying something out of the ordinary.

In the world of Big Data, that "something out of the ordinary" may constitute a single log entry out of millions, which, on its own, may not be worth noticing. But when analyzed against traffic, access, and data flow, that single entry may have untold value and can be a key piece of forensic information. With computer security, seeking anomalies makes a great deal of sense. Nevertheless, many data scientists are reluctant to put much stock in anomalies for other tasks.

Anomalies can actually be the harbingers of trends. Take online shopping, for example, in which many buying trends start off as isolated anomalies created by early adopters of products; these can then transcend into a fad and ultimately become a top product. That type of information—early trending—can make or break a sales cycle. Nowhere is this more true than on Wall Street, where anomalous stock trades can set off all sorts of alarms and create frenzies, all driven by the detection of a few small events uncovered in a pile of Big Data.

Given a large enough data set, anomalies commonly appear. One of the more interesting aspects of anomaly value comes from the realm of social networking, where posts, tweets, and updates are thrown into Big Data and then analyzed. Here businesses are looking at information such as customer sentiment, using a horizontal approach to compare anomalies across many different types of time series, the idea being that different dimensions could share similar anomaly patterns.

Retail shopping is a good example of that. A group of people may do grocery shopping relatively consistently throughout the year at Safeway, Trader Joe's, or Whole Foods but then do holiday shopping at Best Buy and Toys"R"Us, leading to the expected year-end increases. A company like Apple might see a level pattern for most of the year, but when a new iPhone is released, the customers dutifully line up along with the rest of the world around that beautiful structure of glass and steel.

This information translates to the proverbial needle in a haystack that needs to be brought forth above other data elements. It is the concept that for about 300 days of the year, the Apple store is a typical electronics retailer in terms of temporal buying patterns (if not profit margins). However, that all changes when an anomalous event (such as a new product launch) translates into two or three annual blockbuster events, and it becomes the differentiating factor between an Apple store and other electronics retailers. Common trends among industries can be used to discount the expected seasonal variations in order to focus on the truly unique occurrences.

For Twitter data, there are often big disparities among dimensions. Hashtags are typically associated with transient or irregular phenomena, as opposed to, for instance, the massive regularity of tweets emanating from a big country. Because of this greater degree of within-dimension similarity, we should treat the dimensions separately. The dimensional application of algorithms can identify situations in which hashtags and user names, rather than locations and time zones, dominate the list of anomalies, indicating that there is very little similarity among the items in each of these groups.

Given so many anomalies, making sense of them becomes a difficult task, creating the following questions: What could have caused the massive upsurges in the otherwise regular traffic? What domains are involved? Are URL shorteners and Twitter live video streaming services involved? Sorting by the magnitude of the anomaly yields a cursory and excessively restricted view; correlations of the anomalies often exist within and between dimensions. There can be a great deal of synergy among algorithms, but it may take some sort of clustering procedure to uncover them.

EXPEDIENCY VERSUS ACCURACY

In the past, Big Data analytics usually involved a compromise between performance and accuracy. This situation was caused by the fact that technology had to deal with large data sets that often required hours or days to analyze and run the appropriate algorithms on. Hadoop solved some of these problems by using clustered processing, and other technologies have been developed that have boosted performance. Yet real-time analytics has been mostly a dream for the typical organization, which has been constrained by budgetary limits for storage and processing power—two elements that Big Data devours at prodigious rates.

These constraints created a situation in which if you needed answers fast, you would be forced to look at smaller data sets, which could lead to less accurate results. Accuracy, in contrast, often required the opposite approach: working with larger data sets and taking more processing time.

As technology and innovation evolve, so do the available options. The industry is addressing the speed-versus-accuracy problem with in-memory processing technologies, in which data are processed in volatile memory instead of directly on disk. Data sets are loaded into a high-speed cache and the algorithms are applied there, reducing all of the input and output typically needed to read and write to and from physical disk drives.

IN-MEMORY PROCESSING

Organizations are realizing the value of analyzed data and are seeking ways to increase that value even further. For many, the path to more value comes in the form of faster processing. Discovering trends and applying algorithms to process information takes on additional value if that analysis can deliver real-time results.

However, the latency of disk-based clusters and wide area network connections makes it difficult to obtain instantaneous results from BI solutions. The question then is whether real-time processing can deliver enough value to offset the additional expenses of faster technologies. To answer this, one must determine what the ultimate goal of real-time processing is. Is it to speed up results for a particular business process? Is it to meet the needs of a retail transaction? Is it to gain a competitive edge?

The reasons can be many, yet the value gained is still dictated by the price feasibility of faster processing technologies. That is where in-memory processing comes into play. However, there are many other factors that will drive the move toward in-memory processing. For example, a recent study by the *Economist* estimated that humans created about 150 exabytes of information in the year 2005. Although that may sound like an expansive amount, it pales in comparison to the over 1,200 exabytes created in 2011.

Furthermore, the research firm IDC (International Data Corporation) estimates that digital content doubles every 18 months. Further complicating the processing of data is the related growth of unstructured data. In fact, research outlet Gartner projects that as much as 80 percent of enterprise data will take on the form of unstructured elements, spanning traditional and nontraditional sources.

The type of data, the amount of data, and the expediency of accessing the data all influence the decision of whether to use in-memory processing. Nevertheless, these factors might not hold back the coming tide of advanced in-memory processing solutions simply because of the value that in-memory processing brings to businesses.

To understand the real-world advantages of in-memory processing, you have to look at how Big Data has been dealt with to date and understand the current physical limits of computing, which are dictated by the speed of accessing data from relational databases, processing instructions, and all of the other elements required to process large data sets.

Using disk-based processing meant that complex calculations that involved multiple data sets or algorithmic search processing could not happen in real time. Data scientists would have to wait a few hours to a few days for meaningful results—not the best solution for fast business processes and decisions.

Today businesses are demanding faster results that can be used to make quicker decisions and be used with tools that help organizations to access, analyze, govern, and share information. All of this brings increasing value to Big Data.

The use of in-memory technology brings that expediency to analytics, ultimately increasing the value, which is further accentuated by the falling prices of the technology. The availability and capacity per dollar of system memory has increased in the last few years, leading to a repostulation of how large amounts of data can be stored and acted upon.

Falling prices and increased capacity have created an environment where enterprises can now store a primary database in silicon-based main memory, resulting in an exponential improvement in performance and enabling the development of completely new applications. Physical hard drives are no longer the limiting element for expediency in processing.

When business decision makers are provided with information and analytics instantaneously, new insights can be developed and business processes executed in ways never thought possible. In-memory processing signals a significant paradigm shift for IT operations dealing with BI and business analytics as they apply to large data sets.

In-memory processing is poised to create a new era in business management in which managers can base their decisions on real-time analyses of complex business data. The primary advantages are as follows:

- Tremendous improvements in data-processing speed and volume, created by the multifold improvements of data processing, which can amount to hundreds of times of increased performance compared to older technologies.

- In-memory processing that can handle rapidly expanding volumes of information while delivering access speeds that are thousands of times faster than that of traditional physical disk storage.

- Better price-to-performance ratios than can displace the overall costs of in-memory processing, compared to disk-based processing, yet still offer real-time analytics.

- The ability to leverage the significant reductions in the cost of central processing units and memory cost in recent years, combined with multicore and blade architectures, to modernize data operations while delivering measurable results.

In-memory processing offers these advantages and many others by shifting the analytics process from a cluster of hard drives and independent CPUs to a single comprehensive database that can handle all the day-to-day transactions and updates, as well as analytical requests, in real time.

In-memory computing technology allows for the processing of massive quantities of transactional data in the main memory of the server, thereby providing immediate results from the analysis of these transactions.

Since in-memory technology allows data to be accessed directly from memory, query results come back much more quickly than they would from a traditional disk-based warehouse. The time it takes to update the database is also significantly reduced, and the system can handle more queries at a time.

With this vast improvement in process speed, query quality, and business insight, in-memory database management systems promise performance that is 10 to 20 times faster than traditional disk-based models.

The elements of in-memory computing are not new, but they have now been developed to a point where common adoption is possible. Recent improvements in hardware economics and innovations in software have now made it possible for massive amounts of data to be sifted, correlated, and updated in seconds with in-memory technology. Technological advances in main memory, multicore processing, and data management have combined to deliver dramatic increases in performance.

In-memory technology promises impressive benefits in many areas. The most significant are cost savings, enhanced efficiency, and greater immediate visibility of a sort that can enable improved decision making.

Businesses of all sizes and across all industries can benefit from the cost savings obtainable through in-memory technology. Database management currently accounts for more than 25 percent of most companies' IT budgets. Since in-memory databases use hardware systems that require far less power than traditional database management systems, they dramatically reduce hardware and maintenance costs.

In-memory databases also reduce the burden on a company's overall IT landscape, freeing up resources previously devoted to responding to requests for reports. And since in-memory solutions are based on proven mature technology, the implementations are nondisruptive, allowing companies to return to operations quickly and easily.

Any company with operations that depend on frequent data updates will be able to run more efficiently with in-memory technology. The conversion to in-memory technology allows an entire technological layer to be removed from a company's IT architecture, reducing the complexity and infrastructure that traditional systems require. This reduced complexity allows data to be retrieved nearly instantaneously, making all of the teams in the business more efficient.

In-memory computing allows any business user to easily carve out subsets of BI for convenient departmental usage. Work groups can operate autonomously without affecting the workload imposed on a central data warehouse. And, perhaps most important, business users no longer have to call for IT support to gain relevant insight into business data.

These performance gains also allow business users on the road to retrieve more useful information via their mobile devices, an ability that is increasingly important as more businesses incorporate mobile technologies into their operations.

With that in mind, it becomes easy to see how in-memory technology allows organizations to compile a comprehensive overview of their business data, instead of being limited to subsets of data that have been compartmentalized in a data warehouse.

With those improvements to database visibility, enterprises are able to shift from after-event analysis (reactive) to real-time decision making (proactive) and then create business models that are predictive rather than response based. More value can be realized by combining easy-to-use analytic solutions from the start with the analytics platform. This allows anyone in the organization to build queries and dashboards with very little expertise, which in turn has the potential to create a pool of content experts who, without external support, can become more proactive in their actions.

In-memory technology further benefits enterprises because it allows for greater specificity of information, so that the data elements are personalized to both the customer and the business user's individual needs. That allows a particular department or line of business to self-service specific needs whose results can trickle up or down the management chain, affecting account executives, supply chain management, and financial operations.

Customer teams can combine different sets of data quickly and easily to analyze a customer's past and current business conditions using in-memory technology from almost any location, ranging from the office to the road, on their mobile devices. This allows business users to interact directly with customers using the most up-to-date information; it creates a collaborative situation in which business users can interact with the data directly. Business users can experiment with the data in real time to create more insightful sales and marketing campaigns. Sales teams have instant access to the information they need, leading to an entirely new level of customer insight that can maximize revenue growth by enabling more powerful up-selling and cross-selling.

With traditional disk-based systems, data are usually processed overnight, which may result in businesses being late to react to important supply alerts. In-memory technology can eliminate that problem by giving businesses full visibility of their supply-and-demand chains on a second-by-second basis. Businesses are able to gain insight in real time, allowing them to react to changing business conditions. For example, businesses may be able to create alerts, such as an early warning to restock a specific product, and can respond accordingly.

Financial controllers face increasing challenges brought on by increased data volumes, slow data processing, delayed analytics, and slow data-response times. These challenges can limit the controllers' analysis time frames to several days rather than the more useful months or quarters. This can lead to a variety of delays, particularly at the closing of financial periods. However, in-memory technology, large-volume data analysis, and a flexible modeling environment can result in faster-closing financial quarters and better visibility of detailed finance data for extended periods.

In-memory technology has the potential to help businesses in any industry operate more efficiently, from consumer products and retailing to manufacturing and financial services. Consumer products companies can use in-memory technology to manage their suppliers, track and trace products, manage promotions, provide support in complying with Environmental Protection Agency standards, and perform analyses on defective and under-warranty products.

Retail companies can manage store operations in multiple locations, conduct point-of-sale analytics, perform multichannel pricing analyses, and track damaged, spoiled, and returned products. Manufacturing organizations can use in-memory technology to ensure operational performance management, conduct analytics on production and maintenance, and perform real-time asset utilization studies. Financial services companies can conduct hedge fund trading analyses, such as managing client exposures to currencies, equities, derivatives, and other instruments. Using information accessed from in-memory technology, they can conduct real-time systematic risk management and reporting based on market trading exposure.

As the popularity of Big Data analytics grows, in-memory processing is going to become the mainstay for many businesses looking for a competitive edge.

CHAPTER 10

Bringing It All Together

The promises offered by data-driven decision making have been widely recognized. Businesses have been using business intelligence (BI) and business analytics for years now, realizing the value offered by smaller data sets and offline advanced processing. However, businesses are just starting to realize the value of Big Data analytics, especially when paired with real-time processing.

That has led to a growing enthusiasm for the notion of Big Data, with businesses of all sizes starting to throw resources behind the quest to leverage the value out of large data stores composed of structured, semistructured, and unstructured data. Although the promises wrapped around Big Data are very real, there is still a wide gap between its potential and its realization.

That wide gap is highlighted by those who have successfully used the concepts of Big Data at the outset. For example, it is estimated that Google alone contributed $54 billion to the U.S. economy in 2009, a significant economic effect, mostly attributed to the ability to handle large data sets in an efficient manner.

That alone is probably reason enough for the majority of businesses to start evaluating how Big Data analytics can affect the bottom line, and those businesses should probably start evaluating Big Data promises sooner rather than later.

Delving into the value of Big Data analytics reveals that elements such as heterogeneity, scale, timeliness, complexity, and privacy problems can impede progress at all phases of the process that create value from data. The primary problem begins at the point of data acquisition, when the data tsunami requires us to make decisions, currently in an ad hoc manner, about what data to keep, what to discard, and how to reliably store what we keep with the right metadata.

Adding to the confusion is that most data today are not natively stored in a structured format; for example, tweets and blogs are weakly structured pieces of text, while images and video are structured for storage and display but not for semantic content and search. Transforming such content into a structured format for later analysis is a major challenge.

Nevertheless, the value of data explodes when they can be linked with other data; thus data integration is a major creator of value. Since most data are directly generated in digital format today, businesses have the opportunity and the challenge to influence the creation of facilitating later linkage and to automatically link previously created data.

Data analysis, organization, retrieval, and modeling are other foundational challenges. Data analysis is a clear bottleneck in many applications because of the lack of scalability of the underlying algorithms as well as the complexity of the data that need to be analyzed. Finally, presentation of the results and their interpretation by nontechnical domain experts is crucial for extracting actionable knowledge.

THE PATH TO BIG DATA

During the last three to four decades, primary data management principles, including physical and logical independence, declarative querying, and cost-based optimization, have created a multibillion-dollar industry that has delivered added value to collected data. The evolution of these technical advantages has led to the creation of BI platforms, which have become one of the primary tenets of value extraction and corporate decision making.

The foundation laid by BI applications and platforms has created the ideal environment for moving into Big Data analytics. After all, many of the concepts remain the same; it is just the data sources and the quantity that primarily change, as well as the algorithms used to expose the value.

That creates an opportunity in which investment in Big Data and its associated technical elements becomes a must for many businesses. That investment will spur further evolution of the analytical platforms in use and will strive to create collaborative analytical solutions that look beyond the confines of traditional analytics. In other words, appropriate investment in Big Data will lead to a new wave of fundamental technological advances that will be embodied in the next generations of Big Data management and analysis platforms, products, and systems.

The time is now. Using Big Data to solve business problems and promote research initiatives will most likely create huge economic value in the U.S. economy for years to come, making Big Data analytics the norm for larger organizations. However, the path to success is not easy and may require that data scientists rethink data analysis systems in fundamental ways.

A major investment in Big Data, properly directed, not only can result in major scientific advances but also can lay the foundation for the next generation of advances in science, medicine, and business. So business leaders must ask themselves the following: Do they want to be part of the next big thing in IT?

THE REALITIES OF THINKING BIG DATA

Today, organizations and individuals are awash in a flood of data. Applications and computer-based tools are collecting information on an unprecedented scale. The downside is that the data have to be managed, which is an expensive, cumbersome process. Yet the cost of that management can be offset by the intrinsic value offered by the data, at least when looked at properly.

The value is derived from the data themselves. Decisions that were previously based on guesswork or on painstakingly constructed models of reality can now be made based on the data themselves. Such Big Data analysis now drives nearly every aspect of our modern society, including mobile services, retail, manufacturing, financial services, life sciences, and physical sciences.

Certain market segments have had early success with Big Data analytics. For example, scientific research has been revolutionized by Big Data, a prime case being the Sloan Digital Sky Survey, which has become a central resource for astronomers the world over.

Big Data has transformed astronomy from a field in which taking pictures of the sky was a large part of the job to one in which the pictures are all in a database already and the astronomer's task is to find interesting objects and phenomena in the database.

Transformation is taking place in the biological arena as well. There is now a well-established tradition of depositing scientific data into a public repository and of creating public databases for use by other scientists. In fact, there is an entire discipline of bioinformatics that is largely devoted to the maintenance and analysis of such data. As technology advances, particularly with the advent of next-generation sequencing, the size and number of available experimental data sets are increasing exponentially.

Big Data has the potential to revolutionize more than just research; the analytics process has started to transform education as well. A recent detailed quantitative comparison of different approaches taken by 35 charter schools in New York City has found that one of the top five policies correlated with measurable academic effectiveness was the use of data to guide instruction.

This example is only the tip of the iceberg; as access to data and analytics improves and evolves, much more value can be derived. The potential here leads to a world where authorized individuals have access to a huge database in which every detailed measure of every student's academic performance is stored. That data could be used to design the most effective approaches for education, ranging from the basics, such as reading, writing, and math, to advanced college-level courses.

A final example is the health care industry, in which everything from insurance costs to treatment methods to drug testing can be improved with Big Data analytics. Ultimately, Big Data in the health care industry will lead to reduced costs and improved quality of care, which may be attributed to making care more preventive and personalized and basing it on more extensive (home-based) continuous monitoring.

More examples are readily available to prove that data can deliver value well beyond one's expectations. The key issues are the analysis performed and the goal sought. The previous examples only scratch the surface of what Big Data means to the masses. The essential point here is to understand the intrinsic value of Big Data analytics and extrapolate the value as it can be applied to other circumstances.

HANDS-ON BIG DATA

The analysis of Big Data involves multiple distinct phases, each of which introduces challenges. These phases include acquisition, extraction, aggregation, modeling, and interpretation. However, most people focus just on the modeling (analysis) phase.

Although that phase is crucial, it is of little use without the other phases of the data analysis process, which can create problems like false outcomes and uninterruptable results. The analysis is only as good as the data provided. The problem stems from the fact that there are poorly understood complexities in the context of multi-tenanted data clusters, especially when several analyses are being run concurrently.

Many significant challenges extend beyond and underneath the modeling phase. For example, Big Data has to be managed for context, which may include spurious information and can be heterogeneous in nature; this is further complicated by the lack of an upfront model. It means that data provenance must be accounted for, as well as methods created to handle uncertainty and error.

Perhaps the problems can be attributed to ignorance or, at the very least, a lack of consideration for primary topics that define the Big Data process yet are often afterthoughts. This means that questions and analytical processes must be planned and thought out in the context of the data provided. One has to determine what is wanted from the data and then ask the appropriate questions to get that information.

Accomplishing that will require smarter systems as well as better support for those making the queries, perhaps by empowering those users with natural language tools (rather than complex mathematical algorithms) to query the data. The key issue is the level of achievable artificial intelligence and how much that can be relied on. Currently,

IBM's Watson is a major step toward integrating artificial intelligence with the Big Data analytics space, yet the sheer size and complexity of the system precludes its use for most analysts.

This means that other methodologies to empower users and analysts will have to be created, and they must remain affordable and be simple to use. After all, the current bottleneck with processing Big Data really has become the number of users who are empowered to ask questions of the data and analyze them.

THE BIG DATA PIPELINE IN DEPTH

Big Data does not arise from a vacuum (except, of course, when studying deep space). Basically, data are recorded from a data-generating source. Gathering data is akin to sensing and observing the world around us, from the heart rate of a hospital patient to the contents of an air sample to the number of Web page queries to scientific experiments that can easily produce petabytes of data.

However, much of the data collected is of little interest and can be filtered and compressed by many orders of magnitude, which creates a bigger challenge: the definition of filters that do not discard useful information. For example, suppose one data sensor reading differs substantially from the rest. Can that be attributed to a faulty sensor, or are the data real and worth inclusion?

Further complicating the filtering process is how the sensors gather data. Are they based on time, transactions, or other variables? Are the sensors affected by environment or other activities? Are the sensors tied to spatial and temporal events such as traffic movement or rainfall?

Before the data are filtered, these considerations and others must be addressed. That may require new techniques and methodologies to process the raw data intelligently and deliver a data set in manageable chunks without throwing away the needle in the haystack. Further filtering complications come with real-time processing, in which the data are in motion and streaming on the fly, and one does not have the luxury of being able to store the data first and process them later for reduction.

Another challenge comes in the form of automatically generating the right metadata to describe what data are recorded and how they are recorded and measured. For example, in scientific experiments, considerable detail on specific experimental conditions and procedures may be required to be able to interpret the results correctly, and it is important that such metadata be recorded with observational data.

When implemented properly, automated metadata acquisition systems can minimize the need for manual processing, greatly reducing the human burden of recording metadata. Those who are gathering data also have to be concerned with the data provenance. Recording information about the data at their time of creation becomes important as the data move through the data analysis process. Accurate provenance can prevent processing errors from rendering the subsequent analysis useless. With suitable provenance, the subsequent processing steps can be quickly identified. Proving the accuracy of the data is accomplished by generating suitable metadata that also carry the provenance of the data through the data analysis process.

Another step in the process consists of extracting and cleaning the data. The information collected will frequently not be in a format ready for analysis. For example, consider electronic health records in a medical facility that consist of transcribed dictations from several physicians, structured data from sensors and measurements (possibly with some associated anomalous data), and image data such as scans. Data in this form cannot be effectively analyzed. What is needed is an information extraction process that draws out the required information from the underlying sources and expresses it in a structured form suitable for analysis.

Accomplishing that correctly is an ongoing technical challenge, especially when the data include images (and, in the future, video). Such extraction is highly application dependent; the information in an MRI, for instance, is very different from what you would draw out of a surveillance photo. The ubiquity of surveillance cameras and the popularity of GPS-enabled mobile phones, cameras, and other portable devices means that rich and high-fidelity location and trajectory (i.e., movement in space) data can also be extracted.

Another issue is the honesty of the data. For the most part, data are expected to be accurate, if not truthful. However, in some cases, those who are reporting the data may choose to hide or falsify information.

For example, patients may choose to hide risky behavior, or potential borrowers filling out loan applications may inflate income or hide expenses. The list is endless of ways in which data could be misinterpreted or misreported. The act of cleaning data before analysis should include well-recognized constraints on valid data or well-understood error models, which may be lacking in Big Data platforms.

Moving data through the process requires concentration on integration, aggregation, and representation of the data—all of which are process-oriented steps that address the heterogeneity of the flood of data. Here the challenge is to record the data and then place them into some type of repository.

Data analysis is considerably more challenging than simply locating, identifying, understanding, and citing data. For effective large-scale analysis, all of this has to happen in a completely automated manner. This requires differences in data structure and semantics to be expressed in forms that are machine readable and then computer resolvable. It may take a significant amount of work to achieve automated error-free difference resolution.

The data preparation challenge even extends to analysis that uses only a single data set. Here there is still the issue of suitable database design, further complicated by the many alternative ways in which to store the information. Particular database designs may have certain advantages over others for analytical purposes. A case in point is the variety in the structure of bioinformatics databases, in which information on substantially similar entities, such as genes, is inherently different but is represented with the same data elements.

Examples like these clearly indicate that database design is an artistic endeavor that has to be carefully executed in the enterprise context by professionals. When creating effective database designs, professionals such as data scientists must have the tools to assist them in the design process, and more important, they must develop techniques so that databases can be used effectively in the absence of intelligent database design.

As the data move through the process, the next step is querying the data and then modeling it for analysis. Methods for querying and mining Big Data are fundamentally different from traditional statistical analysis. Big Data is often noisy, dynamic, heterogeneous, interrelated, and untrustworthy—a very different informational source from small data sets used for traditional statistical analysis.

Even so, noisy Big Data can be more valuable than tiny samples because general statistics obtained from frequent patterns and correlation analysis usually overpower individual fluctuations and often disclose more reliable hidden patterns and knowledge. In addition, interconnected Big Data creates large heterogeneous information networks with which information redundancy can be explored to compensate for missing data, cross-check conflicting cases, and validate trustworthy relationships. Interconnected Big Data resources can disclose inherent clusters and uncover hidden relationships and models.

Mining the data therefore requires integrated, cleaned, trustworthy, and efficiently accessible data, backed by declarative query and mining interfaces that feature scalable mining algorithms. All of this relies on Big Data computing environments that are able to handle the load. Furthermore, data mining can be used concurrently to improve the quality and trustworthiness of the data, expose the semantics behind the data, and provide intelligent querying functions.

Virulent examples of introduced data errors can be readily found in the health care industry. As noted previously, it is not uncommon for real-world medical records to have errors. Further complicating the situation is the fact that medical records are heterogeneous and are usually distributed in multiple systems. The result is a complex analytics environment that lacks any type of standard nomenclature to define its respective elements.

The value of Big Data analysis can be realized only if it can be applied robustly under those challenging conditions. However, the knowledge developed from that data can be used to correct errors and remove ambiguity. An example of the use of that corrective analysis is when a physician writes "DVT" as the diagnosis for a patient. This abbreviation is commonly used for both deep vein thrombosis and diverticulitis, two very different medical conditions. A knowledge base constructed from related data can use associated symptoms or medications to determine which of the two the physician meant.

It is easy to see how Big Data can enable the next generation of interactive data analysis, which by using automation can deliver real-time answers. This means that machine intelligence can be used in the future to direct automatically generated queries toward Big Data—a key capability that will extend the value of data for automatic content creation for web sites, populate hot lists or recommendations, and to provide an ad hoc analysis of the value of a data set to decide whether to store or discard it.

Achieving that goal will require scaling complex query-processing techniques to terabytes while enabling interactive response times, and currently this is a major challenge and an open research problem. Nevertheless, advances are made on a regular basis, and what is a problem today will undoubtedly be solved in the near future as processing power increases and data become more coherent.

Solving that problem will require a technique that eliminates the lack of coordination among database systems that host the data and provide SQL querying, with analytics packages that perform various forms of non-SQL processing such as data mining and statistical analyses. Today's analysts are impeded by a tedious process of exporting data from a database, performing a non-SQL process, and bringing the data back. This is a major obstacle to providing the interactive automation that was provided by the first generation of SQL-based OLAP systems. What is needed is a tight coupling between declarative query languages and the functions of Big Data analytics packages that will benefit both the expressiveness and the performance of the analysis.

One of the most important steps in processing Big Data is the interpretation of the data analyzed. That is where business decisions can be formed based on the contents of the data as they relate to a business process. The ability to analyze Big Data is of limited value if the users cannot understand the analysis. Ultimately, a decision maker, provided with the result of an analysis, has to interpret these results. Data interpretation cannot happen in a vacuum. For most scenarios, interpretation requires examining all of the assumptions and retracing the analysis process.

An important element of interpretation comes from the understanding that there are many possible sources of error, ranging from processing bugs to improper analysis assumptions to results based on erroneous data—a situation that logically prevents users from fully ceding authority to a fully automated process run solely by the computer system. Proper interpretation requires that the user understands and verifies the results produced by the computer. Nevertheless, the analytics platform should make that easy to do, which currently remains a challenge with Big Data because of its inherent complexity.

In most cases, crucial assumptions behind the data are recorded that can taint the overall analysis. Those analyzing the data need to be aware of these situations. Since the analytical process involves multiple steps, assumptions can creep in at any point, making documentation and explanation of the process especially important to those interpreting the data. Ultimately that will lead to improved results and will introduce self-correction into the data process as those interpreting the data inform those writing the algorithms of their needs.

It is rarely enough to provide just the results. Rather, one must provide supplementary information that explains how each result was derived and what inputs it was based on. Such supplementary information is called the *provenance* of the data. By studying how best to acquire, store, and query provenance, in conjunction with using techniques to accumulate adequate metadata, we can create an infrastructure that provides users with the ability to interpret the analytical results and to repeat the analysis with different assumptions, parameters, or data sets.

BIG DATA VISUALIZATION

Systems that offer a rich palette of visualizations are important in conveying to the users the results of the queries, using a representation that best illustrates how data are interpreted in a particular situation. In the past, BI systems users were normally offered tabular content consisting of numbers and had to visualize the data relationships themselves. However, the complexity of Big Data makes that difficult, and graphical representations of analyzed data sets are more informative and easier to understand.

It is usually easier for a multitude of users to collaborate on the analytical results when it is presented in a graphical form, simply because interpretation is removed from the formula and the users are shown the results. Today's analysts need to present results in powerful visualizations that assist interpretation and support user collaboration.

These visualizations should be based on interactive sources that allow the users to click and redefine the presented elements, creating a constructive environment where theories can be played out and other hidden elements can be brought forward. Ideally, the interface will allow visualizations to be affected by what-if scenarios or filtered by other related information, such as date ranges, geographical locations, or statistical queries.

Furthermore, with a few clicks the user should be able to go deeper into each piece of data and understand its provenance, which is a key feature to understanding the data. Users need to be able to not only see the results but also understand why they are seeing those results.

Raw provenance, particularly regarding the phases in the analytics process, is likely to be too technical for many users to grasp completely. One alternative is to enable the users to play with the steps in the analysis—make small changes to the process, for example, or modify values for some parameters. The users can then view the results of these incremental changes. By these means, the users can develop an intuitive feeling for the analysis and also verify that it performs as expected in corner cases, those that occur outside normal circumstances. Accomplishing this requires the system to provide convenient facilities for the user to specify analyses.

BIG DATA PRIVACY

Data privacy is another huge concern, which increases as one equates such privacy with the power of Big Data. For electronic health records, there are strict laws governing what can and cannot be done. For other data, regulations, particularly in the United States, are less forceful. However, there is great public fear about the inappropriate use of personal data, particularly through the linking of data from multiple sources. Managing privacy is effectively both a technical and a sociological problem, and it must be addressed jointly from both perspectives to realize the promise of Big Data.

Take, for example, the data gleaned from location-based services. A situation in which new architectures require a user to share his or her location with the service provider results in obvious privacy concerns. Hiding the user's identity alone without hiding the location would not properly address these privacy concerns.

An attacker or a (potentially malicious) location-based server can infer the identity of the query source from its location information. For example, a user's location information can be tracked through several stationary connection points (e.g., cell towers). After a while, the user leaves a metaphorical trail of bread crumbs that lead to a certain residence or office location and can thereby be used to determine the user's identity.

Several other types of private information, such as health issues (e.g., presence in a cancer treatment center) or religious preferences (e.g., presence in a church), can also be revealed by just observing anonymous users' movement and usage pattern over time.

Furthermore, with the current platforms in use, it is more difficult to hide a user location than to hide his or her identity. This is a result of how location-based services interact with the user. The location of the user is needed for successful data access or data collection, but the identity of the user is not necessary.

There are many additional challenging research problems, such as defining the ability to share private data while limiting disclosure and ensuring sufficient data utility in the shared data. The existing methodology of differential privacy is an important step in the right direction, but it unfortunately cripples the data payload too severely to be useful in most practical cases.

Real-world data are not static in nature, but they get larger and change over time, rendering the prevailing techniques almost useless, since useful content is not revealed in any measurable amount for future analytics. This requires a rethinking of how security for information sharing is defined for Big Data use cases. Many online services today require us to share private information (think of Facebook applications), but beyond record-level access control we do not understand what it means to share data, how the shared data can be linked, and how to give users fine-grained control over this sharing.

Those issues will have to be worked out to preserve user security while still providing the most robust data set for Big Data analytics.

Appendix

Supporting Data

This appendix contains two white papers:

1. "The MapR Distribution for Apache Hadoop"
2. "High Availability: No Single Points of Failure"

Each paper offers its own take and provides additional knowledge for those looking to leverage Big Data solutions.

WHITE PAPER

The MapR Distribution for Apache Hadoop

Easy, Dependable & Fast Hadoop

TABLE OF CONTENTS

Executive Summary

With the Internet now touching two billion people daily, every call, tweet, e-mail, download, or purchase generates valuable data. Companies are increasingly relying on Hadoop to unlock the hidden value of this rapidly expanding data, and to drive increased growth and profitability. Orbitz has 4.6 million unique site visitors per month. Facebook grew from 400 million users to 500 million users in less than six months. Zynga recently served up 7.5 million virtual Valentine's Day cakes. Each of these companies relies on Hadoop to process massive amounts of data and improve their business.

Hadoop uses are also not limited to analyzing clickstreams. Sensor output, videos, log files, location data, genomics, behavioral data, and seismic studies are just a few of the data sources that are driving Hadoop use across government agencies and business verticals. At the same time, experienced users understand the challenges and limitations presented by Hadoop. While there is currently a choice of six different Hadoop distributions, they all share the same configuration issues, single points of failure, data loss risks, and performance limitations.

This paper provides details on a significant new alternative — the MapR Distribution for Apache Hadoop — the easiest, most dependable, and fastest Hadoop distribution.

Strategic Hadoop

In evaluating and selecting a Hadoop distribution, organizations need to choose criteria that mean the most to their business or activity. Key questions related to the distribution include:

- **How easy is it to use?**
  How easily does data move into and out of the cluster?
  Can the cluster be easily shared across users, workloads, and geographies?
  Can the cluster easily accommodate access, protection, and security while supporting large numbers of files?

- **How dependable is the Hadoop cluster?**
  Can it be trusted for production and business-critical data?
  How does the distribution help ensure business continuity?
  Can the cluster recover data from user and application errors?
  Can data be mirrored between different clusters?

- **How does it perform?**
  Is processing limited to batch applications?
  Does the namenode create a performance bottleneck?
  Does the system use hardware efficiently?

MapR's innovations allow more businesses to harness the power of Big Data analytics. These technological advances make Hadoop easier, more dependable, and significantly faster, vastly broadening the scope of how and where Hadoop can be used.

127

A Complete, Advanced, Hadoop Distribution

The MapR Distribution for Apache Hadoop adds innovation to the excellent work already done by a large community of developers. With key new technology advances, MapR transforms Hadoop into a dependable and interactive system with real-time data flows.

The MapR Distribution for Apache Hadoop is 100% API compatible with Apache Hadoop including MapReduce, HDFS, and HBase. MapR fully tests and supports the complete distribution, combining MapR's intellectual property with the best of the best from the community, including the latest patches. As shown in Figure 1, MapR provides the entire Hadoop stack, including:

- Language access components (Hive and Pig)
- Database components (HBase)
- Workflow management libraries (Oozie)
- Application building libraries (Mahout)
- SQL to Hadoop database import/export (Sqoop)
- Log collection (Flume)
- The entire MapReduce layer
- Underlying storage services functionality

Overcoming the limitations of other Hadoop distributions, the MapR distribution is designed to scale efficiently from a single node to tens of thousands of nodes with petabytes of data.

Figure 1. The MapR Distribution for Apache Hadoop is 100% compatible with Apache Hadoop, and adds multiple ease of use, dependability, and performance innovations.

EASIER HADOOP

In order for Hadoop to be effective for broader groups of users and larger workloads, it must be easy to use, provision, operate, and manage at scale. MapR has invested in developing key breakthroughs that make it much easier to move data into and out of the cluster, provision cluster resources, and manage even very large Hadoop clusters with a small staff.

MOVING FROM BATCH TO REAL-TIME DATA FLOWS

Other Hadoop distributions manage data through a cumbersome batch process that slows data processing. The application first logs data to direct or network-attached storage. On some pre-determined time interval, data is then batch loaded into traditional Apache Hadoop's write-once file system. Finally, analytics are then run to create a result set, and those results are then batch-unloaded for further analysis.

The standard batch process causes a significant time lag between data production by the application and analysis in the Hadoop cluster. Loading data at a higher frequency minimizes this time lag, but results in a large number of small files that can easily challenge the scalability limits of traditional Hadoop. Other Hadoop distributions are also limited by the write-once Hadoop Distributed File System (HDFS). Like a conventional CD-ROM, HDFS prevents files from being modified once they have been written, and files cannot be read before they are closed.

In sharp contrast, MapR Direct Access™ NFS enables real-time read/write data flows via the industry-standard Network File System (NFS) protocol. With MapR Direct Access NFS, any remote client can simply mount the cluster. Application servers can write their log files and other data directly into the cluster, rather than writing it first to direct- or network-attached storage. Enabled by MapR Lockless Storage Services, MapR Direct Access NFS makes Hadoop radically easier and less expensive to use:

- Unlike the write-once system found in traditional Hadoop, the MapR distribution allows files to be modified, overwritten, and read as required. MapR Lockless Storage Services enable multiple concurrent reads and writes on any file.

- Graphical file browsers can be used to access and manipulate cluster data. Users can simply browse files, automatically open associated applications with a mouse click, or drag-and-drop files and directories into and out of the cluster.

- Files in the cluster can be edited directly by text editors and integrated development environments (IDEs).

- Standard command-line tools and UNIX applications and utilities (such as Grep, Sed, Tar, Sort, and Tail) can be used directly on data in the cluster. With other Hadoop distributions, the user must either develop their own tools, or copy the data out of the cluster in order to use standard tools.

- The MapR distribution greatly reduces the need for log collection tools (such as Flume) that often require agents on every application server. Application servers can either write data directly into the cluster or use standard tools like Rsync to synchronize data between local disks and the cluster.

- Application binaries, libraries, and configuration files can be stored inside the cluster and accessed directly, greatly simplifying operation.

BUILT-IN COMPRESSION

While data compression can be done with traditional Hadoop distributions, it is difficult and inefficient. Data is typically compressed manually before copying it into the cluster and a special MapReduce job is then run to index the compressed data (assuming parallelism is desired in the application). Applications must also be modified so that they can consume the compression indices.

The MapR Distribution for Apache Hadoop provides automatic compression that offers both performance acceleration and significant storage savings. MapR's compression saves both network I/O bandwidth and storage footprint.

MULTIPLE CLUSTER SUPPORT

It is often useful for organizations to operate multiple Hadoop clusters, whether to separate different data or applications, or for business continuity, or for performance. The MapR Distribution for Apache Hadoop is inherently designed to work with multiple clusters and provides direct access, remote mirroring, and multi-cluster management.

- **Direct access.** All MapR Hadoop clusters can be accessed directly and easily from both inside and outside of Hadoop. For example, if an organization has two clusters named "dev" and "test", then files on the dev cluster would be available under */mapr/dev* whereas files in the test cluster would be under */mapr/test*. These paths are identical whether the system is accessed through the Hadoop cluster (*hadoop fs -ls /mapr/dev/user/jdoe*) or remotely through NFS (*ls /mapr/dev/user/jdoe*). In addition, files can easily be copied between clusters with a simple copy command (*cp /mapr/dev/foo.txt /mapr/test/*). Symbolic links can easily be configured across clusters.

- **Remote mirroring.** The MapR distribution can be easily configured to mirror data between clusters using MapR Mirroring. This capability can be used for business continuity (by mirroring data to another cluster), or to keep a production and research clusters in sync.

- **Multi-cluster management.** All clusters running the MapR distribution of Apache Hadoop are visible through the MapR Control System (MCS). A user can easily view and switch between available clusters.

PROVISIONING, OPERATING, AND MANAGING THE CLUSTER

As data analysis needs grow, so does the need to effectively manage and utilize expensive cluster resources. Making data manageable at scale presents a significant challenge, both in terms of locating and accessing data, and in terms of applying policies to that data. Cluster infrastructure must accommodate many applications, users, and departments, and administrators need effective ways to apply policy to very large numbers of files. Cluster applications and data must also be provisioned in line with both technical needs and business-driven priorities.

Typical provisioning questions for enterprise applications might include:
- How much CPU capacity is needed (now and in the future)?
- How much storage is needed (now and in the future)?
- Will the applications require high I/O storage?
- What are the data protection requirements?
- What are the business continuity requirements?
- What security authorization and access control methods are required?

Answering these questions in a MapReduce context requires a Hadoop distribution with considerable depth and agility. Other Hadoop distributions require that policies (such as ownership, replication, etc.) be managed at the file level — a virtually impossible task given the potential for millions of files. The MapR Distribution for Apache Hadoop provides enterprise-class features and advanced data management functionality that lets organizations meet the business-level objectives outlined above simply, easily, and economically.

MapR Volumes

MapR Volumes make cluster data both easy to access and easy to manage by grouping related files and directories into a single tree structure so they can be easily organized, managed, and secured. MapR volumes provide the ability to apply policies including the following:

- *Replication.* The replication factor determines how many replicas of the data exist throughout the cluster.

- *Snapshots.* MapR Snapshots allow for online point-in-time data recovery without costly replication of data. A volume snapshot is consistent (atomic), does not copy data, and does not impact performance.

- *Mirroring.* MapR Mirroring allows for load balancing, cross-cluster backup, bulk data transfer, and failover for continuity. Local mirroring provides high performance for highly accessed data, while remote mirroring provides business continuity and integration between on-premise and private clouds.

- *Quotas.* Quotas allow organizations to accurately manage the needs of the application, user, or department by limiting the disk space for any user, group, or volume, and "charging" a volume to a specific user or group. The MapR Distribution for Apache Hadoop provides quotas for storage capacity within the cluster. Quotas can be configured on an individual volume or on a user or group. Over-quota email notifications can be sent automatically. Users and groups can come from the local system, or from standard name services such as NIS or LDAP.

- *Data placement control.* The MapR Distribution for Apache Hadoop allows data to be placed as desired within the cluster. For example, applications with significant I/O requirements could have their data placed on high-speed media such as SSDs, with other data placed on standard disk devices.

- *Administration permissions.* In some environments, a cluster administrator may want to delegate administration rights to others. Administrative permissions can be granted to allow specific users to create and remove volumes, perform mirroring and snapshots, and set quotas.

- *Data access.* User access to data can be established at the volume level. MapR integrates with standard directory services such as LDAP or NIS.

Easy Administration at Scale

At the scale of large Hadoop clusters, visibility and automation are essential. Administrators simply do not have the time to troubleshoot and manage servers individually. Advanced data management and self-healing capabilities make it easy for an individual administrator to manage a MapR cluster with thousands of nodes.

The MapR Distribution for Apache Hadoop includes the following to make administration easy:
- A complete, tested Hadoop stack pre-integrated with numerous components such as Hive, Pig, Oozie, etc.
- Simple installation
- Complete management through GUI, CLI, and REST APIs
- Rolling upgrades and downgrades with no downtime

The MapR Control System (MCS) provides full visibility into cluster resources and activity. As shown in Figure 2, the MCS includes the MapR Hadoop Heatmap™ that provides visual insight into node health, service status, and resource utilization, organized by cluster topology (e.g., datacenters and racks). Designed to manage large clusters with thousands of nodes, the MapR Hadoop Heatmap shows the health of the entire cluster at a glance. Filters and group actions are also provided to select specific components and perform administrative actions directly since the number of nodes, files, and volumes can be very high.

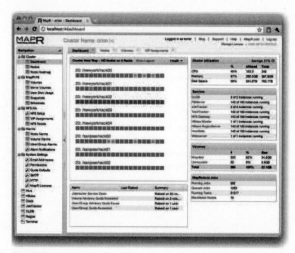

Figure 2. The MapR Hadoop Heatmap provides instant insights into the status of all nodes in each cluster.

Dependable Hadoop

Dependability is essential for business continuity, and enterprise organizations have demanding expectations in terms of reliability, availability, and storage functionality — particularly with regard to production data. Unlike other distributions, the MapR distribution features a distributed-everything architecture, functioning as an enterprise-ready cluster and trusted data store that is safe for shared environments:

- **High availability.** Everything in the MapR distribution is transactional, journaled and logged, and able to restart in seconds. The entire cluster is self-healing and self-tuning. The JobTracker and NameNode have been re-engineered to be distributed and replicated. NFS HA means that clients won't hang waiting for unavailable servers. Rolling upgrades make sure that the cluster is always available.

- **Data protection.** Unlike traditional Hadoop distributions, there are no single points of failure and a minimum of three-fold replication is provided for cluster metadata. The system guards against silent data corruption, and end-to-end checksums are performed all the way from the memory of the client through to the disk in the cluster. MapR Snapshots provide point-in-time recovery images while MapR Mirroring offers business continuity through both remote and local mirroring to protect data.

- **Disaster recovery.** Remote mirroring provides the capability to keep a synchronized copy of cluster data at a remote site, so that business operations can continue uninterrupted in the case of a disaster. Management of multiple on-site or geographically-dispersed clusters is simple with the MapR Control System.

- **A safe, shared environment.** The MapR distribution protects system resources against runaway jobs. MapR assures that no application can inadvertently take resources from the core cluster. In other distributions, a bug in a user job (such as an infinite loop) can impact critical system daemons.

- **Monitoring.** Filtered alarms and notifications are provided at many levels, including cluster-wide, per-service, per-volume, per user and group, and per-node with support for e-mail groups. Usage tracking and quotas help administrators effectively track and charge for resources. Integration with third-party monitoring systems is also provided.

Eliminating Lost Jobs

The Hadoop JobTracker keeps track of large numbers of Mappers and Reducers distributed across the cluster. Unfortunately, the JobTracker provided in other distributions runs only on a single node, and represents a single point of failure for the entire cluster. If the JobTracker fails, all running jobs fail and all progress is lost. In addition, administrators must first detect this situation in other Hadoop distributions, and then manually restart the JobTracker.

The MapR JobTracker HA improves recovery time objectives and provides for a self-healing cluster. Upon failure, the MapR JobTracker automatically restarts on another node in the cluster. TaskTrackers will automatically pause and then reconnect to the new JobTracker. Any currently running jobs or tasks continue without losing any progress or failing.

Distributed NameNode for HA and Scale

In Hadoop, the NameNode tracks where all the data is located in the cluster. In other Hadoop distributions, the NameNode runs on a single server, even for very large clusters which creates several problems. The MapR distribution provides a Distributed NameNode that eliminates these shortcomings.

- *No Single point of failure.* A single NameNode results in a single point of failure. If the name node goes down, the entire cluster becomes unavailable, requiring minutes or hours to restart the NameNode. With MapR, every node in the cluster stores and serves metadata, so that there is no loss or downtime even in the face of multiple disk or node failures.

- *An unlimited number of files.* Even with an exceptionally powerful server, the NameNode in other Hadoop distributions is limited to only about 70 million files. To attempt to work around this issue, many large Hadoop sites actively run Hadoop jobs to walk through the cluster and concatenate files — amounting to a significant percentage of their daily jobs and wasting both resources and money. MapR's distributed NameNode scales linearly with the number of nodes, eliminating the file limit.

- *Performance advantage.* In other Hadoop distributions, all metadata operations (e.g. lookups, creates) in the cluster have to go through a single NameNode, limiting performance. This shortcoming both impacts performance and restricts the workloads that can run on the cluster. With MapR, every node in the cluster stores and serves metadata, resulting in high performance that scales with the size of the cluster.

High Availability, Direct Loading for Hadoop

MapR provides several innovations that make NFS access useful and reliable. High availability (HA) has been implemented using virtual IP addresses, making Hadoop suitable for production environments. Multiple cluster nodes (up to every node in the cluster) can be designated as NFS gateways, and MapR manages failures transparently. Load balancing can be configured so that client connections are uniformly distributed among all of the NFS gateways. In addition, MapR allows NFS clients to control chunk size (e.g., 64 MB, 128 MB, 256 MB) and compression settings via a hidden pseudo-file in each directory (similar to */proc* files in Linux).

Snapshots for Easy Data Recovery

With the significant amounts of data being collected for processing today, true backups are often impractical. At the same time, organizations absolutely need the ability to revert their data to a specific point in time in the case of application corruption or user error. Replication is the only form of data protection offered by other Hadoop distributions. Unfortunately, replication only protects from disk and node failures, but does not protect from user and application errors since those errors are replicated throughout the cluster. Many Hadoop users have lost valuable data due to these errors.

MapR Snapshots let organizations address their recovery point objectives by providing a point-in-time recovery image that protects from user and application errors. MapR Snapshots can be scheduled or performed on demand, and they can be managed through the MapR Control System. MapR Snapshots operate on MapR Volumes. Recovering from a snapshot is as easy as browsing the snapshot directory and copying the directory or file to the current directory. Snapshots can be performed on individual volumes independently, and different volumes can have different schedules.

Complex schedules can be defined. For example, a snapshot schedule for "critical data" could entail:

- An hourly snapshot taken and retained for 24 hours.
- A daily snapshot taken at 12am, and retained for 7 days.
- A weekly snapshot taken on Sunday at 12am and retained for 12 weeks.

MapR Snapshots offer high performance and space efficiency and provide a number of distinct advantages.

- *Fast performance.* No data is copied in order to create a snapshot. As a result, a snapshot of a petabyte volume can be performed in seconds.

- *Atomic.* Snapshot operations are atomic and fully consistent.

- *No impact on write performance.* A snapshot operation does not have any impact on write performance. MapR uses redirect-on-write operations, meaning that each write in the system goes to a new block on disk. Redirect-on-write operations are more efficient than copy-on-write operations.

- *Minimal storage usage.* Snapshots do not consume any disk space until files are modified or deleted. Any unmodified blocks are shared between the snapshots and the current read/write image of the volume. As a result, MapR's snapshots use the minimum possible disk space, offering fast distributed snapshots with zero performance loss on writing to the original. Easy recovery is offered by simply copying a file from the snapshot.

MIRRORING

Many organizations need to create physical point-in-time copies of their data. To address this requirement, MapR provides mirroring that can be used in two distinct forms. Remote mirroring (described in this section) provides mirroring between clusters for disaster-recovery, development/test, or private-public cloud integration. Local mirroring (described in the section on performance) can be used for load balancing and performance enhancements within the same cluster. Remote mirroring can facilitate numerous use cases.

- *Disaster recovery (DR).* With remote mirroring, organizations can deploy a secondary cluster for disaster recovery purposes — typically in a different datacenter or different geographic area. Data can then be recovered from the secondary cluster in the event of data loss. Moreover, entire applications can fail over to the secondary cluster if a disaster impacts the primary cluster.

- *Research cluster.* With MapR, organizations can easily deploy a research (or dev/test) cluster alongside their production cluster. The administrator simply creates mirrored volumes on the research cluster, and the system periodically mirrors the data from the production cluster to the research cluster. This capability allows users of the research cluster to operate on real, up-to-date data.

- *Private-public cloud integration.* While most organizations choose to run Hadoop on their own hardware infrastructure, some may find it useful to occasionally launch an additional cluster in the public cloud (e.g., Amazon EC2) for extra compute capacity. For example, an organization might decide to launch a 100-node cluster on EC2 every Friday night to address a special processing need. MapR makes it easy to synchronize data between a local cluster and a cluster in the public cloud.

- *Efficiency.* MapR mirrors are differential, meaning that only deltas are transferred from the source to the destination. For example, if only a single 8 KB block in a file has been modified since the previous mirroring operation, only that block will be transmitted in the next mirror. All data is compressed on the wire to expedite transfer and checksums are used to ensure integrity. When more than one mirror of a volume is desired, mirrors can be cascaded to minimize transmission bandwidth needs. Data is transferred asynchronously and in parallel by the servers providing the source volume, and does not impact local system performance.

- *Network or sneakernet.* If there is too much data to mirror over a network connection, the mirror can be dumped to one or more portable disks or servers at the source location, and then physically shipped and loaded at the destination (so-called "sneakernet mirroring"). Network and sneakernet mirroring can interoperate. For example, a large data mirror can be created at the source cluster, shipped to a remote location, and then bulk loaded and synced over the network with the remote cluster.

- *Atomic operation.* MapR Mirroring is based on MapR Snapshots, inheriting atomic operations. No change occurs on the destination cluster until all of the data has been received for a given mirroring operation. The destination cluster is then updated atomically. Mirroring relationships can be configured and monitored through the GUI, CLI or REST API. A mirroring schedule (similar to a snapshot schedule) can be set up at a volume level.

Faster Hadoop

From the beginning, the MapR Distribution for Apache Hadoop was designed to provide significant I/O and performance advantages. MapR offers enhanced performance on clusters of any size, from a single node to thousands.

Architected for Performance

From the outset, the MapR distribution has been re-designed for performance, with architectural advancements at all levels, including:

- *MapR Lockless Storage Services.* MapR Lockless Storage Services accelerate MapReduce performance and provide multi-dimensional scalability. Data routing tables are used rather than mutexes or spinlocks in the implementation, eliminating lock contention. State machines are used rather than threads, reserving thread resources for executing user applications that share the nodes. MapR Lockless Storage Services write directly to block devices rather than through HDFS or Linux file system layers.

- *Optimized shuffle.* MapR's shuffle takes advantage of MapR Lockless Storage Services for shuffling data between Mappers and Reducers. As a result, when the Reducers read the Mapper outputs, the data is read from disk sequentially (potentially across multiple disks), resulting in very high performance. The optimized MapR shuffle does not utilize the Linux page cache, and thus avoids competing with user applications for precious memory resources. The result is a shuffle that is typically three times faster than other distributions.

- *Distributed NameNode.* Other Hadoop distributions rely on a single NameNode for all metadata operations for the entire cluster. In contrast, the MapR Distributed NameNode distributes metadata operations across all cluster nodes, yielding orders of magnitude greater scalability.

- *Built-in compression.* Data is transparently compressed with the MapR distribution, saving disk and network I/O.

- *Implementation language.* The lower layers of the MapR distribution are written in the C/C++ language. Beyond higher efficiency and performance, this implementation choice also overcomes the garbage collection issues that impact other distributions.

- *Multi-NIC support.* Most servers today are equipped with at least two network interface controllers (NICs). The MapR distribution can utilize multiple network interface controllers (NICs) on each node via NIC bonding, without requiring port trunking at the switch level. From the network perspective, only one socket is opened between any two peers in the MapR Hadoop cluster.

- *Minimal CPU/memory footprint.* Since MapReduce applications run on the same nodes as file services in Hadoop clusters, MapR set out to minimize the CPU and memory footprint of the infrastructure itself. A minimal footprint preserves CPU, memory, and other resources for application processing. In addition, all MapR services are implemented as user-space processes — yielding performance benefits without compromising stability.

Performance-Related Features

Beyond the architectural advantages of MapR's implementation, data placement control and local mirroring are provided to customize Hadoop implementations and increase performance.

- *Data placement control.* The MapR distribution provides data placement control, unlike other Hadoop distributions that offer no control over where data is physically stored in the cluster. Data placement control can be used to set the policy on a volume to restrict that volume to a subset of the available nodes. A volume could be restricted to nodes in a specific rack or datacenter, or to nodes with a specific hardware configuration. For example, an application with a randomly and frequently-accessed session lookup table could have the MapR Volume containing the lookup table restricted to the nodes in the cluster equipped with SSD drives, thus resulting in much higher performance.

- *Local mirroring and Mirror Volumes.* MapReduce spawns large numbers of processes that often access the same data. With traditional Hadoop technology, these simultaneous accesses to a single file system element can quickly overwhelm file servers and slow performance, particularly at job startup. With local mirroring (also known as Mirror Volumes) multiple copies of a volume can be created. The copies are updated asynchronously, and all copies are accessed through the same path. The system automatically load balances the read requests between these copies.

Performance Testing

MapR has done performance testing to compare and evaluate the performance of the MapR Distribution for Apache Hadoop with other distributions. Results in the categories of streaming I/O, random I/O, and MapReduce performance are provided in the sections that follow.

137

STREAMING I/O PERFORMANCE

As one of the first standard benchmarks for I/O performance in a Hadoop context, the DFSIO benchmark provides a useful metric to gauge streaming I/O performance. The benchmark is a MapReduce job with multiple mappers and a single reducer. The key measurement is the transfer rate (in MB/s) for an average mapper. For this test, MapR engineers evaluated DFSIO on a 10-node cluster (Figure 3).

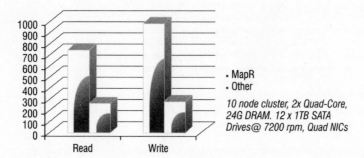

Figure 3. The DFSIO benchmark (larger is better) performs three times faster on the MapR Distribution for Apache Hadoop than on traditional Apache Hadoop.

The systems used in the 10-node cluster for this test featured two quad-core processors, 24 GB of RAM, and twelve 1 TB 7200 RPM SATA disk drives. As the chart illustrates, I/O was basically running at the physical limitation of the hardware for the MapR distribution. The CPU was basically idle during these tests, attesting to efficient data paths. Write speed in the test is slightly slower due to checksum computations.

RANDOM I/O PERFORMANCE

Some applications require the ability to create and address large numbers of files. To evaluate performance in this area, MapR engineers tested the MapR Distribution for Apache Hadoop against traditional Hadoop with a variation on the standard NNBench test that performs the following steps repeatedly:

- Create a file
- Write 100 bytes to the file
- Close the file

The application was run on the same 10-node cluster configured with both traditional Apache Hadoop and the MapR distribution. Block reports were disabled on traditional Apache Hadoop to allow completion of the test. The results of the test are shown in Figure 4.

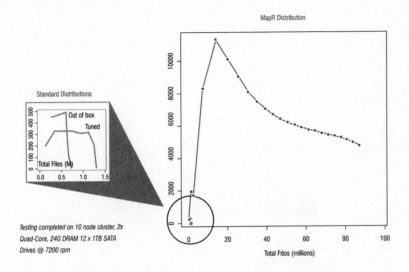

Figure 4. The MapR Distribution for Apache Hadoop outperforms traditional Apache Hadoop for random I/O.

The MapR Distribution for Apache Hadoop demonstrated dramatically better results in both rate (vertical axis) and volume (horizontal axis). In fact, the disparity is so large that the traditional Apache Hadoop results have to be magnified to even be visible. Even with block reports turned off, traditional Apache Hadoop was able to store less than 1.5 million files before the rate dropped precipitously. In contrast, the MapR distribution was able to write 90 million files total at rates of 12,000 declining to 4,000 files per second. These results demonstrate a sixty-fold scalability factor.

MapReduce Performance

Beyond I/O, engineers wanted to evaluate the data analysis performance of the MapR distribution. The Terasort benchmark was run on a 10-node cluster, with each node comprised of two quad-core processors, 24 GB of RAM, and twelve 1 TB SATA disk drives. The results of the benchmark test are shown in Figure 5.

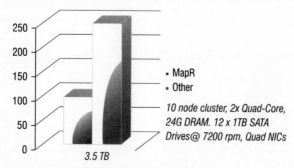

Figure 5. The MapR Distribution for Apache Hadoop provides almost three times the performance of traditional Hadoop in the Terasort benchmark (smaller is better).

ATTRIBUTE	APACHE HADOOP	MAPR DISTRIBUTION FOR APACHE HADOOP
Cluster Size	1-3,000	1-10,000+
Maximum Data in Cluster	20 PB	1,000 PB
Maximum Files	70 Million	1 Trillion
Volumes	—	200,000
Performance	1x	3x to 20x
Infrastructure Footprint	1x	50% Smaller

Table 1 compares scalability between the MapR distribution and other Apache Hadoop distributions.

140

CONCLUSION

MapR believes that the increasing criticality of data processing demands a strategic focus on the choice of Hadoop platform. While other distributions are already available, only the MapR Distribution for Apache Hadoop provides a demonstrable difference and addresses other Hadoop shortcomings and limitations (Table 2). The MapR Distribution for Apache Hadoop provides unique features and functionality that simply are not available with any other Hadoop distribution, including:

- Simple installation, provisioning and manageability for cluster visibility and ease of use
- Enterprise-class dependability, storage access, and storage management
- Breakthrough performance leading to cost containment through drastically lower hardware requirements

MapR's investments and innovations make Hadoop easy, dependable, and fast for today's most demanding applications — while providing Hadoop infrastructure that is ready for the challenges to come.

CRITERIA	TRADITIONAL APACHE HADOOP	MAPR DISTRIBUTION FOR APACHE HADOOP
Completeness	No	Yes. Includes popular tools. Does not require expensive external backup storage
Performance	1x	3x to 20x performance improvement, data placement control, and optimized shuffle
Cost of Hardware	1x	1/2x and first-year ROI
Scalability (files)	70 Million	Unlimited number of files. MapR Distributed Name Node for scalability
Ease of Operation	No	MapR Heatmap, GUI, Alarms and filters
Continuous data load and access to results	No	MapR Direct Access NFS for MapR Realtime Hadoop
Dependability and Business Continuity	No	MapR JobTracker HA, MapR Distributed NameNode, MapR Snapshots for point-in-time recovery, MapR Mirroring for disaster recovery
Reliable sharing of the cluster	No	Alerts, alarms, quotas, users, groups, and system resource isolation
Provisioning & usage tracking	No	MapR Volumes, quotas, and users
Multi-datacenter	No	MapR Mirroring across clusters and datacenters. Manage multiple clusters from a single GUI
Support	Available	Yes

Table 2 The MapR Distribution Advantages

MapR Technologies is the creator of the industry's fastest, most dependable and easiest to use distribution for Apache Hadoop. MapR Technologies is dedicated to advancing the Hadoop platform and ecosystem to enable more businesses to harness the power of big data analytics for competitive advantage. For more information, please visit www.mapr.com.

HIGH AVAILABILITY: NO SINGLE POINTS OF FAILURE

TABLE OF CONTENTS

EXECUTIVE SUMMARY

The MapR Distribution for Apache Hadoop provides high availability with no single points of failure across the entire stack. In the storage layer, MapR's Distributed NameNode HA™ architecture provides high availability with self-healing and support for multiple, simultaneous failures, with no additional hardware whatsoever. In the MapReduce layer, MapR's JobTracker HA makes JobTracker failures transparent to applications – the currently running tasks continue to execute during the failover process. In the NFS layer, MapR automatically manages virtual IP addresses and balances them between the nodes so that failures are transparent to clients that are reading and writing data via NFS. (Note that NFS support is not available in any other distribution.)

These capabilities, combined with MapR's unique capabilities for data protection (snapshots) and disaster recovery (mirroring), position MapR as the only distribution that provides business continuity. By comparison, Apache Hadoop 0.21 and prior versions, and the corresponding commercial distributions such as Cloudera's Distribution including Apache Hadoop (CDH) also do not provide any HA capabilities. Furthermore, future versions of Apache Hadoop through 2012 will provide only limited HA, with many architectural issues and limitations. The following table outlines the key differences in business continuity between MapR, Apache Hadoop 0.20 and the planned releases of Apache Hadoop 0.23/0.24:

	MapR	Apache Hadoop 0.21 and Prior Versions	Future Release: Apache Hadoop 0.23/0.24
Storage HA			
HA architecture	**Distributed**	None (single point of failure)	*Active / Passive*
# of failures tolerated	**Unlimited**	0	*1*
Self-healing	**Scalability (files)**	No	No
Dedicated hardware needed for metadata	**0**	2 servers (NameNode, Checkpoint/Backup Node) + NAS (e.g., NetApp)	2+ servers + NAS (e.g., NetApp)
Additional servers needed to store 1 billion files	**0**	Can't scale beyond 50-100M files in a cluster!	20-40 high-end servers w/ HDFS Federation
Automated rolling upgrades	**Yes**	No	No
MapReduce HA			
HA architecture	**Active / Passive**	None (single point of failure)	**Active / Passive**
Task failures	**No Tasks Fail**	All Tasks Fail	*Running tasks fail*
NFS HA			
HA architecture	**Distributed (automatic VIP failover)**	No NFS access to data	No NFS access to data
Data Protection			
HA architecture	Yes	Yes	Yes
Snapshots for recovery from user/application errors	Yes	No	No
Mirroring for disaster recovery and remote backup	Yes	No	No
Availibile Today	**Yes**	**Yes**	No — expected 2012 release

Background

One of the capabilities that differentiate MapR from other Hadoop distributions is high availability (HA). With the MapR Distribution for Hadoop, there are no single points of failure, so any component can fail with no impact to the user, jobs or administrator. This document describes the HA capabilities of MapR's storage services and MapReduce framework. Note that MapR also provides complete HA for the NFS access layer, as well as HBase.

We asked many Hadoop users about their HA requirements. The following requirements were the most common:

1) **No downtime or data/job loss on failure.** In other words, an individual hardware or software failure should not have any impact on applications.

2) **Self-healing.** The cluster should automatically heal from a failure so that it can tolerate additional failures in the future. No human intervention should be required after a failure. Some failures (e.g., disk failure) obviously require intervention, but in a self-healing architecture, intervention is not required in order to recover from a failure and restore to a highly available state, assuming there are enough physical resources available.

3) **Tolerate multiple failures.** The cluster should be able to tolerate more than one simultaneous failure. Ideally, the degree of tolerance should be configurable so that the administrator or user can choose the appropriate re source level to support how many failures can be tolerated (e.g., production data is probably more important than temporary scratchpad data).

4) **No additional hardware.** There should be no need to purchase, deploy and maintain additional hardware (e.g., nodes).

5) **100% commodity hardware.** There should be no dependency on non-commodity hardware, such as hardware load balancers or network-attached storage (e.g., NetApp).

6) **Easy to set up.** It should be trivial to set up HA. For example, the administrator should not need to install any third-party software or hardware (commercial or open source).

The driving factors behind these requirements are a combination of increasing the level of protection (mean time to failure, or MTTF) and making it easy to deploy and maintain. Hadoop users love the fact that they don't have to attend to a DataNode failure until they have time, and expect that type of guarantee for every service.
The following sections describe the high availability architecture of the MapR distribution, and how it compares with the current state and roadmap of other distributions and projects.

144

STORAGE

MapR

MapR's Lockless Storage Services feature a distributed HA architecture:

- The metadata is distributed across the entire cluster. Every node stores and serves a portion of the metadata.

- Every portion of the metadata is replicated on three different nodes (this number can be increased by the administrator). For example, the metadata corresponding to all the files and directories under /project/ advertising would exist on three nodes. The three replicas are consistent at all times except, of course, for a short time after a failure.

- The metadata is persisted to disk, just like the data.

The following illustration shows how metadata is laid out in a MapR cluster (in this case, a small 8-node cluster). Each colored triangle represents a portion of the overall metadata; or in MapR terminology, the metadata of a single volume is:

In this example each portion of the metadata is on three different nodes, so the system can tolerate two failures without a problem. Increasing the number of replicas for the metadata of a volume is as simple as modifying the value in a textbox in the MapR Control System, or running a command via the CLI or REST API.

If a node fails, the metadata that was on that node is quickly re-replicated to other nodes in the cluster so that the replication factor can quickly hit the configured level again. This is what makes MapR's HA self-healing. Note that all nodes in the cluster can participate in the healing process, making it extremely efficient. The following list outlines one possible chain of events that could take place if FileServer 6 (in the preceding example) crashes:

1) FileServer 1 copies the "yellow" metadata from FileServer 3
2) FileServer 2 copies the "green" metadata from FileServer 4
3) FileServer 3 copies the "purple" metadata from FileServer 7

It is worth noting that enabling HA in MapR's lockless storage services does not require any effort. By default, all metadata is replicated three times, just like the regular data. In addition, there is no need to deploy additional nodes or any non-commodity hardware.

Other distributions

MapR is currently the only distribution that provides HA. There have been a number of projects that attempted to increase the availability of Hadoop clusters, but neither these projects nor the existing roadmap address the majority of the preceding HA requirements. This section provides more details on the existing Hadoop distributions as well as three related projects: AvatarNode, Linux HA/DRBD and NameNode HA (the latter has not been implemented).

Apache Hadoop 0.21 and prior versions (including CDH)

In other Hadoop distributions, all HDFS metadata (e.g., namespace, block locations) is kept in memory on a single node, called the NameNode. In addition, the NameNode typically stores the namespace information on both a local disk and a non-commodity NAS system (e.g., NetApp), while block locations are maintained solely in memory.

If the NameNode fails, the entire cluster is down. Furthermore, since the NameNode doesn't keep block locations on disk, the NameNode must reconstruct the information from all the DataNodes. This can take hours.

The following illustration outlines the architecture of HDFS. Each colored triangle represents a portion of the metadata, and the grey rectangles represent block locations. As you can see, the metadata is stored on a single machine, and it must fit entirely in memory.

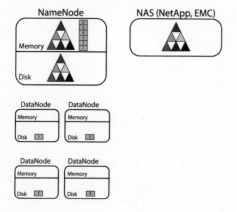

Note that HDFS includes a service called the Secondary NameNode. This service runs on a separate node, and its job is to merge the NameNode's edit log into the fsimage so that the edit log does not grow indefinitely (this would cause a NameNode restart to take forever). It is important to keep in mind that the Secondary NameNode cannot become a Primary NameNode, and thus does not provide any form of HA. Because the term Secondary NameNode is misleading, this service was renamed Checkpoint Node in Hadoop 0.21. In addition, an alternative service called Backup Node was introduced in 0.21. The Backup Node serves the same role as the Checkpoint Node, but is able to checkpoint more efficiently (because the edits are continuously streamed from the NameNode to the Backup Node, instead of being downloaded periodically).

LINUX HA/DRBD

Linux HA and DRBD have been used in the past by a few Hadoop users to improve the availability of their Hadoop clusters. This solution employs a standby NameNode that is ready to assume responsibility when the active NameNode fails. However, this approach has several problems. For example, the standby NameNode is cold, so the cluster could be down for a significant amount of time (e.g., over an hour) following a NameNode failure, waiting for the backup NameNode to read (and merge) the file system image and edit log, and then waiting to receive a block report from every DataNode in the cluster.

Although this solution was originally described in Cloudera's own blog, the company later commented that "... we want to clarify our position that we do not officially support nor fully endorse this method of doing NameNode HA. DRBD is hard to get right, and you can easily corrupt your fsimage file with a subtle mistake. ... our recommendation is to design your application around HDFS's availability semantics. This might include using Flume for reliable delivery, or having mirrored HDFS systems."

To summarize, the Linux HA/DRBD solution does not meet any of the six preceding HA requirements.

AVATARNODE

AvatarNode, developed by Facebook, makes it possible for an administrator to switch a live Hadoop cluster's NameNode from one node to another node so that the administrator can then perform maintenance on the node. The failover must be manually initiated by an administrator, so it doesn't provide protection from software or hardware failures, and does not meet any of the six preceding HA requirements.

With that said, AvatarNode is important to Facebook because the company is maintaining its own internal version of Hadoop, and has the need to upgrade the Hadoop software on a frequent basis. The AvatarNode project makes it possible to perform minor upgrades to the NameNode with no downtime.

APACHE HADOOP 0.23/0.24 (NAMENODE HA AND HDFS FEDERATION)

NameNode HA is another HA-related project that aims to add high availability to HDFS. It is described in umbrella JIRA HDFS-1623. NameNode HA is still in the design phase. At a high level, the idea is to actively replicate all NameNode state required to quickly restart the process. There are still many open questions, so it's not clear what the design will be, but it will likely be an extension of AvatarNode. None of the proposals provide self-healing or the ability to tolerate multiple failures. In addition, the proposals all require a dedicated standby server, and most likely a commercial NAS system. The illustration to the right outlines the proposed architecture.

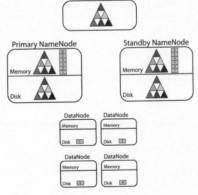

Note that even under the proposed NameNode HA architecture, all metadata must reside in memory on the NameNode. As a result, a cluster with one Primary NameNode and one Standby NameNode can only support about 50-100M files (similarly to an Apache Hadoop 0.20/0.21 cluster). To address this limitation, a project called HDFS Federation is being developed. HDFS Federation allows administrators to divide the namespace between multiple NameNodes. HDFS Federation doesn't provide any HA (in fact, it introduces multiple single points of failure), but it does provide some relief for the "# of files" limit in Hadoop. However, it does so at an extremely high cost:

- HDFS Federation introduces multiple single points of failure (each of the NameNodes is a single point of failure), unless the customer deploys a dedicated Standby NameNode for each of those NameNodes. However, that doubles the hardware and associated costs. For example, to store 1B files in a cluster, one would need to deploy 10-20 Primary NameNodes, and 10-20 Standby NameNodes, for a total of 20-40 dedicated NameNode servers! A cluster with 10B files would require 200-400 dedicated NameNode servers. Compare that to a MapR cluster, which would require zero additional servers to scale to many billions of files (and beyond).

- Any time a new NameNode is added, the configuration on every client and DataNode must be updated. This is because HDFS Federation requires clients to share a common mount table

MapReduce

MapR

MapR is the only distribution that provides JobTracker high availability. When the JobTracker fails, the system automatically restarts the JobTracker on a different node, and the TaskTrackers automatically reconnect to the new JobTracker. All MapReduce jobs continue to run during this time. In fact, even the tasks that are in flight are not affected by the failure. This is important because losing all the running tasks in a MapReduce job can be almost as disruptive as losing the entire job (i.e., both the tasks that have completed, and the ones that are still running). MapR's JobTracker HA is designed to meet all six of the preceding HA requirements. During the deployment phase, the administrator can decide which machines are candidates for running the JobTracker. At any point in time, one of the available candidates serves as the active JobTracker. Therefore, the MapReduce layer can tolerate an arbitrary number of simultaneous failures, and the administrator does not need to intervene. Also, no additional hardware is needed, and enabling JobTracker HA is as simple as running a single command on each candidate node.

In terms of high availability, MapReduce 2.0 offers a subset of the capabilities of MapR's JobTracker HA. When the MapReduce ApplicationMaster (i.e., the job-specific JobTracker) fails, it is restarted automatically, but all incomplete map/reduce tasks must be restarted.

OTHER DISTRIBUTIONS

APACHE HADOOP 0.21 AND PRIOR VERSIONS (INCLUDING CDH)

Apache Hadoop 0.20 and 0.21 do not have any high availability for the JobTracker. If the JobTracker fails, all running jobs are terminated and their progress is lost. This can be a serious problem especially in a scenario in which jobs must complete within a specific timeframe.

APACHE HADOOP 0.23 (MAPREDUCE 2.0)

MapReduce 2.0 is a new architecture for MapReduce that was proposed by Yahoo!, and closely resembles the architecture that Google uses internally. MapReduce 2.0 provides various benefits, such as scalability, backward compatibility and higher cluster utilization (because it eliminates the need for predefined map and reduce slots). MapR is currently integrating MapReduce 2.0 into the MapR Distribution for Apache Hadoop, so that MapR users can take advantage of these benefits as soon as the community-driven work on the MapReduce 2.0 framework is completed. MapReduce 2.0 will be available in the MapR distribution within four weeks of its general availability in Apache Hadoop or CDH (these four weeks will allow MapR the time to run the system through the company's rigorous QA processes).

CONCLUSION

The MapR Distribution for Apache Hadoop, unlike all other distributions, was designed from the ground up to provide high availability and other business continuity capabilities, such as data protection and disaster recovery. MapR is the only distribution with no single points of failure. Other distributions are expected to introduce limited HA capabilities in 2012, but due to fundamental architectural limitations they are unable to address the most important availability and ease of use requirements. In addition, they will require significant hardware and operating expenses just to tolerate a single failure.

MapR Technologies is the creator of the industry's fastest, most dependable and easiest to use distribution for Apache Hadoop. MapR Technologies is dedicated to advancing the Hadoop platform and ecosystem to enable more businesses to harness the power of big data analytics for competitive advantage. For more information, please visit www.mapr.com.

© 2011. MapR. Confidential. v1 08.11

About the Author

Frank J. Ohlhorst is an award-winning technology journalist, professional speaker, and IT business consultant with over 25 years of experience in the technology arena. Frank has written for several leading technology publications, including *ComputerWorld*, *TechTarget*, *CRN*, *Network Computing*, *PCWorld*, *ExtremeTech*, and *Tom's Hardware*. Frank has contributed to business publications, including *Entrepreneur* and *BNET*, and to multiple technology books. He has written several white papers, case studies, reviewers' guides, and channel guides for leading technology vendors.

Index